POPE
JOHN XXIII

POPE JOHN XXIII

Timothy Walch

1987
CHELSEA HOUSE PUBLISHERS
NEW YORK
NEW HAVEN   PHILADELPHIA

PROJECT EDITOR: John W. Selfridge
ASSOCIATE EDITOR: Marian W. Taylor
EDITORIAL COORDINATOR: Karyn Gullen Browne
EDITORIAL STAFF: Maria Behan
          Karen Dreste
          Pierre Hauser
          Perry Scott King
          Kathleen McDermott
          Howard Ratner
          Alma Rodriguez-Sokol
          Bert Yaeger
LAYOUT: Irene Friedman
ART ASSISTANTS: Noreen Lamb
          Carol McDougall
          Victoria Tomaselli
COVER ILLUSTRATION: Kye Carbone
PICTURE RESEARCH: Karen Herman

Frontispiece courtesy of Associated Press

First Printing

Library of Congress Cataloging-in-Publication Data

Walch, Timothy. POPE JOHN XXIII.

(World leaders past & present)
Bibliography: p.
Includes index.
    1. John XXIII, Pope, 1881–1963—Juvenile
literature. 2. Popes—Biography—Juvenile
literature. [1. John XXIII, Pope, 1881–1963. 2.
Popes] I. Title. II. Series.
BX1378.2.W35   1986   282'.092'4 [B] [92] 86-13719

ISBN 0-87754-535-9

Contents

CHELSEA HOUSE PUBLISHERS

WORLD LEADERS PAST & PRESENT

ADENAUER
ALEXANDER THE GREAT
MARC ANTONY
KING ARTHUR
ATATÜRK
ATTLEE
BEGIN
BEN-GURION
BISMARCK
LÉON BLUM
BOLÍVAR
CESARE BORGIA
BRANDT
BREZHNEV
CAESAR
CALVIN
CASTRO
CATHERINE THE GREAT
CHARLEMAGNE
CHIANG KAI-SHEK
CHURCHILL
CLEMENCEAU
CLEOPATRA
CORTÉS
CROMWELL
DANTON
DE GAULLE
DE VALERA
DISRAELI
EISENHOWER
ELEANOR OF AQUITAINE
QUEEN ELIZABETH I
FERDINAND AND ISABELLA
FRANCO

FREDERICK THE GREAT
INDIRA GANDHI
MOHANDAS GANDHI
GARIBALDI
GENGHIS KHAN
GLADSTONE
GORBACHEV
HAMMARSKJÖLD
HENRY VIII
HENRY OF NAVARRE
HINDENBURG
HITLER
HO CHI MINH
HUSSEIN
IVAN THE TERRIBLE
ANDREW JACKSON
JEFFERSON
JOAN OF ARC
POPE JOHN XXIII
LYNDON JOHNSON
JUÁREZ
JOHN F. KENNEDY
KENYATTA
KHOMEINI
KHRUSHCHEV
MARTIN LUTHER KING, JR.
KISSINGER
LENIN
LINCOLN
LLOYD GEORGE
LOUIS XIV
LUTHER
JUDAS MACCABEUS
MAO ZEDONG

MARY, QUEEN OF SCOTS
GOLDA MEIR
METTERNICH
MUSSOLINI
NAPOLEON
NASSER
NEHRU
NERO
NICHOLAS II
NIXON
NKRUMAH
PERICLES
PERÓN
QADDAFI
ROBESPIERRE
ELEANOR ROOSEVELT
FRANKLIN D. ROOSEVELT
THEODORE ROOSEVELT
SADAT
STALIN
SUN YAT-SEN
TAMERLANE
THATCHER
TITO
TROTSKY
TRUDEAU
TRUMAN
VICTORIA
WASHINGTON
WEIZMANN
WOODROW WILSON
XERXES
ZHOU ENLAI

ON LEADERSHIP
Arthur M. Schlesinger, jr.

LEADERSHIP, it may be said, is really what makes the world go round. Love no doubt smooths the passage; but love is a private transaction between consenting adults. Leadership is a public transaction with history. The idea of leadership affirms the capacity of individuals to move, inspire, and mobilize masses of people so that they act together in pursuit of an end. Sometimes leadership serves good purposes, sometimes bad; but whether the end is benign or evil, great leaders are those men and women who leave their personal stamp on history.

Now, the very concept of leadership implies the proposition that individuals can make a difference. This proposition has never been universally accepted. From classical times to the present day, eminent thinkers have regarded individuals as no more than the agents and pawns of larger forces, whether the gods and goddesses of the ancient world or, in the modern era, race, class, nation, the dialectic, the will of the people, the spirit of the times, history itself. Against such forces, the individual dwindles into insignificance.

So contends the thesis of historical determinism. Tolstoy's great novel *War and Peace* offers a famous statement of the case. Why, Tolstoy asked, did millions of men in the Napoleonic wars, denying their human feelings and their common sense, move back and forth across Europe slaughtering their fellows? "The war," Tolstoy answered, "was bound to happen simply because it was bound to happen." All prior history predetermined it. As for leaders, they, Tolstoy said, "are but the labels that serve to give a name to an end and, like labels, they have the least possible connection with the event." The greater the leader, "the more conspicuous the inevitability and the predestination of every act he commits." The leader, said Tolstoy, is "the slave of history."

Determinism takes many forms. Marxism is the determinism of class. Nazism the determinism of race. But the idea of men and women as the slaves of history runs athwart the deepest human instincts. Rigid determinism abolishes the idea of human freedom—

the assumption of free choice that underlies every move we make, every word we speak, every thought we think. It abolishes the idea of human responsibility, since it is manifestly unfair to reward or punish people for actions that are by definition beyond their control. No one can live consistently by any deterministic creed. The Marxist states prove this themselves by their extreme susceptibility to the cult of leadership.

More than that, history refutes the idea that individuals make no difference. In December 1931 a British politician crossing Park Avenue in New York City between 76th and 77th Streets around 10:30 P.M. looked in the wrong direction and was knocked down by an automobile—a moment, he later recalled, of a man aghast, a world aglare: "I do not understand why I was not broken like an eggshell or squashed like a gooseberry." Fourteen months later an American politician, sitting in an open car in Miami, Florida, was fired on by an assassin; the man beside him was hit. Those who believe that individuals make no difference to history might well ponder whether the next two decades would have been the same had Mario Constasino's car killed Winston Churchill in 1931 and Giuseppe Zangara's bullet killed Franklin Roosevelt in 1933. Suppose, in addition, that Adolf Hitler had been killed in the street fighting during the Munich *Putsch* of 1923 and that Lenin had died of typhus during World War I. What would the 20th century be like now?

For better or for worse, individuals do make a difference. "The notion that a people can run itself and its affairs anonymously," wrote the philosopher William James, "is now well known to be the silliest of absurdities. Mankind does nothing save through initiatives on the part of inventors, great or small, and imitation by the rest of us—these are the sole factors in human progress. Individuals of genius show the way, and set the patterns, which common people then adopt and follow."

Leadership, James suggests, means leadership in thought as well as in action. In the long run, leaders in thought may well make the greater difference to the world. But, as Woodrow Wilson once said, "Those only are leaders of men, in the general eye, who lead in action. . . . It is at their hands that new thought gets its translation into the crude language of deeds." Leaders in thought often invent in solitude and obscurity, leaving to later generations the tasks of imitation. Leaders in action—the leaders portrayed in this series—have to be effective in their own time.

And they cannot be effective by themselves. They must act in response to the rhythms of their age. Their genius must be adapted, in a phrase of William James's, "to the receptivities of the moment." Leaders are useless without followers. "There goes the mob," said the French politician hearing a clamor in the streets. "I am their leader. I must follow them." Great leaders turn the inchoate emotions of the mob to purposes of their own. They seize on the opportunities of their time, the hopes, fears, frustrations, crises, potentialities. They succeed when events have prepared the way for them, when the community is awaiting to be aroused, when they can provide the clarifying and organizing ideas. Leadership ignites the circuit between the individual and the mass and thereby alters history.

It may alter history for better or for worse. Leaders have been responsible for the most extravagant follies and most monstrous crimes that have beset suffering humanity. They have also been vital in such gains as humanity has made in individual freedom, religious and racial tolerance, social justice and respect for human rights.

There is no sure way to tell in advance who is going to lead for good and who for evil. But a glance at the gallery of men and women in *World Leaders—Past and Present* suggests some useful tests.

One test is this: do leaders lead by force or by persuasion? By command or by consent? Through most of history leadership was exercised by the divine right of authority. The duty of followers was to defer and to obey. "Theirs not to reason why,/ Theirs but to do and die." On occasion, as with the so-called "enlightened despots" of the 18th century in Europe, absolutist leadership was animated by humane purposes. More often, absolutism nourished the passion for domination, land, gold and conquest and resulted in tyranny.

The great revolution of modern times has been the revolution of equality. The idea that all people should be equal in their legal condition has undermined the old structure of authority, hierarchy and deference. The revolution of equality has had two contrary effects on the nature of leadership. For equality, as Alexis de Tocqueville pointed out in his great study *Democracy in America*, might mean equality in servitude as well as equality in freedom.

"I know of only two methods of establishing equality in the political world," Tocqueville wrote. "Rights must be given to every citizen, or none at all to anyone . . . save one, who is the master of all." There was no middle ground "between the sovereignty of all and the absolute power of one man." In his astonishing prediction of 20th-century totalitarian dictatorship, Tocqueville explained how the revolution of equality could lead to the *"Führerprinzip"* and more terrible absolutism than the world had ever known.

But when rights are given to every citizen and the sovereignty of all is established, the problem of leadership takes a new form, becomes more exacting than ever before. It is easy to issue commands and enforce them by the rope and the stake, the concentration camp and the *gulag*. It is much harder to use argument and achievement to overcome opposition and win consent. The Founding Fathers of the United States understood the difficulty. They believed that history had given them the opportunity to decide, as Alexander Hamilton wrote in the first Federalist Paper, whether men are indeed capable of basing government on "reflection and choice, or whether they are forever destined to depend . . . on accident and force."

Government by reflection and choice called for a new style of leadership and a new quality of followership. It required leaders to be responsive to popular concerns, and it required followers to be active and informed participants in the process. Democracy does not eliminate emotion from politics; sometimes it fosters demagoguery; but it is confident that, as the greatest of democratic leaders put it, you cannot fool all of the people all of the time. It measures leadership by results and retires those who overreach or falter or fail.

It is true that in the long run despots are measured by results too. But they can postpone the day of judgment, sometimes indefinitely, and in the meantime they can do infinite harm. It is also true that democracy is no guarantee of virtue and intelligence in government, for the voice of the people is not necessarily the voice of God. But democracy, by assuring the right of opposition, offers built-in resistance to the evils inherent in absolutism. As the theologian Reinhold Niebuhr summed it up, "Man's capacity for justice makes democracy possible, but man's inclination to injustice makes democracy necessary."

A second test for leadership is the end for which power is sought. When leaders have as their goal the supremacy of a master race or the promotion of totalitarian revolution or the acquisition and exploitation of colonies or the protection of greed and privilege or the preservation of personal power, it is likely that their leadership will do little to advance the cause of humanity. When their goal is the abolition of slavery, the liberation of women, the enlargement of opportunity for the poor and powerless, the extension of equal rights to racial minorities, the defense of the freedoms of expression and opposition, it is likely that their leadership will increase the sum of human liberty and welfare.

Leaders have done great harm to the world. They have also conferred great benefits. You will find both sorts in this series. Even "good" leaders must be regarded with a certain wariness. Leaders are not demigods; they put on their trousers one leg after another just like ordinary mortals. No leader is infallible, and every leader needs to be reminded of this at regular intervals. Irreverence irritates leaders but is their salvation. Unquestioning submission corrupts leaders and demands followers. Making a cult of a leader is always a mistake. Fortunately hero worship generates its own antidote. "Every hero," said Emerson, "becomes a bore at last."

The signal benefit the great leaders confer is to embolden the rest of us to live according to our own best selves, to be active, insistent, and resolute in affirming our own sense of things. For great leaders attest to the reality of human freedom against the supposed inevitabilities of history. And they attest to the wisdom and power that may lie within the most unlikely of us, which is why Abraham Lincoln remains the supreme example of great leadership. A great leader, said Emerson, exhibits new possibilities to all humanity. "We feed on genius. . . . Great men exist that there may be greater men."

Great leaders, in short, justify themselves by emancipating and empowering their followers. So humanity struggles to master its destiny, remembering with Alexis de Tocqueville: "It is true that around every man a fatal circle is traced beyond which he cannot pass; but within the wide verge of that circle he is powerful and free; as it is with man, so with communities."

—*New York*

1

Formative Years

An air of excitement filled St. Peter's Square outside the Vatican palace in Rome. Tens of thousands of men, women, and children were waiting anxiously for news of the next pope. For three days the cardinals of the Catholic church had been trying to select such a leader. What was taking so long? No one outside the meeting had any knowledge of what was going on inside. By tradition, these meetings of the cardinals, called conclaves, were held in strict secrecy. The visitors to St. Peter's Square, as well as hundreds of millions of Catholics around the world, would have to be patient.

Finally, late on the afternoon of October 28, 1958, a wisp of white smoke appeared from the chimney of the palace chapel. It was the traditional sign that a new pope had been elected. The crowd shifted its attention to the main balcony of the palace. At half past six the doors of the balcony opened and out came a procession of Vatican officials followed by a short, stocky man dressed in white. *"Habemus papam,"* announced one Vatican official to the crowd. "We have a pope." *"Viva papa,"* responded the crowd in unison, "Long live the pope." Little did anyone realize that the man who stood before them,

> *When one is elevated to the supreme pontiff's office, that person no longer belongs to himself, to one people, or to a single nation. He then belongs to all peoples whom the Catholic church reaches and embraces.*
> —CARDINAL ANTONIO BACCI

Angelo Giuseppe Roncalli (middle) with two fellow students in 1904 while studying for the priesthood in Rome. Roncalli took the first steps towards becoming a priest in 1893, at the seminary in Bergamo. He was ordained a priest on August 10, 1904, in Rome.

Angelo Roncalli, now known as Pope John XXIII, would be responsible for the most sweeping changes in Roman Catholicism in more than four centuries.

On November 25, 1881, in the small village of Sotto il Monte in northern Italy, a poor farmer named Giovanni Batista (John Baptist) Roncalli waited nervously for word of the birth of his fourth child. After three girls, he prayed for a son. When he heard the robust cries of a healthy infant, he asked his wife, "Is it a boy?" "Yes," answered Marianna Roncalli, "you have your son." Giovanni thanked the Lord; someday he would have help in the fields. Little did this poor farmer realize that his beloved first son would become pope of the Roman Catholic church.

The birth of another Roncalli was cause for celebration. The Roncalli clan had lived in Sotto il Monte for more than 300 years and there were many aunts, uncles, and cousins to join in the celebration. But first the child must be baptized. The head of the

Santa Maria Bambina, the small parish church in Sotto il Monte, Italy, where Roncalli was baptized. The church dates to 1480, and the name means "the baby Holy Mary." Roncalli celebrated his first public Mass here in August 1904.

AP/WIDE WORLD

14

clan, Zevario Roncalli, took the baby to the local parish church where the child was baptized Angelo Giuseppe Roncalli. Uncle Zevario was the godfather.

Zevario and Angelo returned home and the baby was incorporated into the life of a large, active household. In addition to Angelo, his parents, his sisters, and Uncle Zevario, the household included an assortment of relatives — and six cows. At the time Angelo was born there were at least 31 other Roncallis in the household. This type of living arrangement was typical for rural Italian families in the 19th century.

Although the Roncallis had lived in Sotto il Monte for a very long time and had prospered in numbers, the clan had never escaped poverty. For centuries Roncalli men had worked as tenant farmers, called *mezzardi* in Italian, renting land from local noblemen. The Roncallis cultivated the land, grew grapes, and divided the crops with their landlords. It was a hard and precarious life. Many years later, after he had become pope, Angelo joked that "there [were] three ways of ruining yourself — wine, women, and farming. My father chose the dullest." There was much truth in his humor.

The poverty of the Roncallis was most evident in their threadbare clothing and their meager diets. "There was never any bread on our table," young Angelo recalled in a letter to his family, "only polenta [a dish made of corn flour]; no wine for the children or the young people; only at Christmas and Easter did we have a slice of homemade cake. Clothes and shoes for going to church had to last years and years." The memory of this poverty stayed with Angelo all of his life.

Although they were poor, the Roncallis were typical of the families in Sotto il Monte and other northern Italian villages. Most of the men were tenant farmers who scratched out a meager life and concerned themselves only with their crops, their families, and their villages. They were an independent and isolated people, largely unaware of events in other parts of Italy or the rest of Europe.

To appreciate the isolation of villages such as Sotto il Monte it is important to know that Italy as

Angelo Roncalli's father and mother, Giovanni Batista and Marianna Mazzola Roncalli. The Roncalli clan had been tenant farmers in the area around Bergamo for centuries. Tenant farming was difficult, but as Pope John XXIII was to say in later years, "we had the necessities of life, and we were strong and healthy."

Italian farmers bringing in grain with ox-drawn wagons. Young Angelo Roncalli showed more aptitude for schoolwork than farming, and was put in the hands of a parish priest, who guided him toward the priesthood.

we know it did not become a nation until 1870. Up to that time it was a collection of independent kingdoms, duchies, city-states, and foreign provinces. For centuries the villagers of Sotto il Monte showed their loyalty only to the city of Bergamo, a trading center about 10 miles to the east, and to Venice, the powerful city-state that dominated the region. The patriotism of the Roncalli family was at the most provincial and rarely national.

This pride of place was impressed upon Angelo from an early age. Throughout his life he closely identified himself with his family, his village, and the city of Bergamo. In later years, no matter where

he was living, he always spent his summers in a villa in Sotto il Monte. And he took delight in all things Bergamese — its literature, its landscape, its food, its music, and its art. Angelo Roncalli, one historian noted, was "Bergamese to the bone."

Although Angelo was proud of his heritage, he showed no interest in farming. In fact, he was of little use to anyone in the household. Exasperated and disappointed, Giovanni Roncalli turned his son over to the local schoolmaster. Perhaps the boy could learn a trade. It proved to be a fateful decision because Angelo showed real aptitude for school-work. Angelo Roncalli, age seven, was a scholar of promise.

In an effort to expand the boy's horizons, the schoolmaster sent Angelo to the village priest, Father Francisco Rebuzinni, for special instruction. The young boy and the old priest were a perfect match. Angelo enjoyed listening to the priest tell stories about the history of the Church and the lives of the saints. In turn, Father Rebuzinni was flattered to have the undivided attention of such a bright young boy.

Through daily lessons Angelo came to admire the priest greatly. After giving the matter serious thought, he expressed an interest in studying for the priesthood. The priest agreed to help and sent the boy to study Latin with a neighboring scholar. At the age of nine, Angelo became a day student at a school six miles away from his home. The long walk and the strict discipline were too much. Angelo quit after less than a year, seemingly defeated. But Father Rebuzinni stepped in, counseled his young pupil, and tutored him for entrance into the local seminary at Bergamo. With Father Rebuzinni's support, Angelo was back on track.

Angelo arrived at the Bergamo seminary in November 1893, shortly before his 12th birthday. He would never falter in his effort to become a priest. This is not to say that Angelo was sure of himself. In fact, the young peasant boy from Sotto il Monte was full of self-doubt. Was he good enough to be one of God's annointed priests? Angelo was not sure.

This self-doubt is evident in a journal, *Journal of*

> *In the summers an excellent preacher, a Jesuit, would talk to us about the eternal truths. And if he were talking about Purgatory, he would shout "Fire! Fire!" This would bring the barber and other shopkeepers in the stores below running into the Piazza Sant'Apollinaire.*
> —JOHN XXIII
> recalling his days
> at seminary

a Soul, that Angelo began in 1895. The early entries are very immature, little more than copies of devotional prayers. But by his final year in the seminary he was wrestling with some very personal, philosophical issues. "Who am I?" he wrote in 1900, "Where am I going? I am nothing. Everything I possess, my being, life, understanding, will, and memory — all are given me by God, so all belongs to Him." Angelo prayed that his faith would drive away the uncertainty of the future.

His doubts about the future did not temper Angelo's proud self-image. During the school year he lived an exalted life remote from the world of his family. When he returned home on vacations, Angelo was shocked by his family's common way of life. "Only three days of vacation have passed," he wrote in his journal, "and already I am weary of them." They, in turn, accused him of snobbery and false pride. Even though he returned to Sotto il Monte every year, he knew that he was different from the rest of the village.

Angelo's academic achievement in the Bergamo seminary led to a scholarship at a theological college in Rome. It was a world far different from anything that Angelo had ever experienced, even in Bergamo. "We live like lords!" he wrote his parents with naive enthusiasm. "In fact, they tell me that I look different already and grow fatter every day." For the first time in his life he had luxuries such as a private room, a chest of drawers, and indoor plumbing. He was overwhelmed.

Angelo was intimidated by his professors, his classmates, and the curriculum. No longer the star pupil of a small diocesan seminary, he gained the reputation in Rome of being a hardworking but undistinguished student, who easily followed the guidance of others but made little effort to think for himself. "It will always be my principle," he wrote in December 1903, "to find out first of all the traditional teaching of the Church, and on this basis to judge the findings of contemporary scholarship."

After an education that was interrupted by a year of compulsory military service, Angelo Roncalli finally reached his goal. On August 10, 1904, he was

> *A priest is supposed to comfort and enlighten souls, and he is able to fulfill this mission because he himself feels the weight of human frailty.*
> —JOHN XXIII
> journal entry written soon
> after his ordination

The Bridge of Sighs, in Venice, Italy. Venice is in northern Italy, the area Roncalli would always consider home. After many years Roncalli returned to Venice, at the age of 71, as archbishop.

EUROPE 1914

NORWAY
SWEDEN
DENMARK
ENGLAND
HOLLAND
BELGIUM
GERMANY
RUSSIA
FRANCE
SWITZ.
AUSTRIA-
HUNGARY
ROMANIA
SPAIN
ITALY
SERBIA
BULGARIA
CORSICA
MONTE
NEGRO
ALBANIA
SARDINIA
GREECE
SICILY

A map of Europe in 1914, just before the start of World War I. Note the absence of Poland, Czechoslovakia, and Yugoslavia, which didn't exist as nations at the time. Roncalli, serving as secretary to Bishop Radini Tedeschi in Bergamo, was called into service in the Italian Army in May 1915.

ordained in the Church of Santa Maria in Monte Santo, Rome. After 11 years of study, he was finally a priest of the Roman Catholic church.

What plans did the bishop of Bergamo have for this ambitious young man? This was the very question that Angelo asked himself the week before his ordination. He did not have to wait long for an answer. His reputation as a hard worker caught the attention of Giacomo Radini Tedeschi, the newly appointed bishop of Bergamo. He was in need of a secretary and young Father Roncalli seemed to be the perfect choice.

Father Roncalli spent 10 tumultuous years in the service of his bishop, and during those years the two men became like father and son. Together they modernized many diocesan institutions. They refurbished the cathedral, built a new home for the bishop, and revised the seminary curriculum. They also established social organizations to aid the poor and distressed of the diocese. As if this were not enough, Roncalli also taught church history at the seminary and began to edit a scholarly edition of the diaries of St. Charles Borromeo. Father Roncalli was a busy young man.

But this wonderful life came crashing down in the summer of 1914. War swept through Europe in August, but that was of little immediate concern to Roncalli: Bishop Radini Tedeschi, the man who had been Roncalli's mentor and friend for the previous decade, lay on his deathbed. The bishop's death on August 22 was one of the saddest moments of Roncalli's life. "I have entered a new period in my life," he wrote prophetically in his journal. Little did he realize how much his world would change.

For the first few months after Radini Tedeschi's death, Father Roncalli contented himself with his teaching and his scholarship. He awaited the arrival of a new bishop and a new assignment. But before this could happen, Roncalli was called into the service of the Italian army as a hospital orderly. Italy had joined the "Great War," now known as World War I, in May 1915. Roncalli, who had risen to the rank of sergeant during his year of compulsory military training in 1902, was a logical candidate for military service. Once again, Angelo Roncalli was required to trade in his clerical garb for a military uniform.

Roncalli's first two and one-half years of service were relatively tranquil. At the time of his induction he had been worried that he would be sent to the front, but, to his relief, he was assigned to a hospital in Bergamo, far from the fighting. During these years he counseled others, particularly his younger brothers, on the obligations of military service. "My

An Italian infantryman in campaign uniform. The fighting in World War I evolved into a bloody stalemate of trench warfare, with tremendous casualties for both the German and Italian armies. Roncalli served as an orderly in a military hospital in Bergamo, tending the wounded soldiers who came from the front.

advice to you is this," he wrote to his brother Zevario in the summer of 1916, "be patient and be a good soldier as long as you can."

During these years the war was a stalemate. The Allies (Great Britain, France, Italy, Russia, and the United States) fought the Central Powers (Germany, the Austro-Hungarian Empire, and the Ottoman Empire) with little exchange of territory. But in October 1917 the Austrians mounted an offensive that drove the Italian army back 70 miles to within 15 miles of Venice. The refugees and war-wounded streamed into the army hospital at Bergamo. "We must pray to the Lord that He may bless our dear country," Roncalli wrote to his brother in November, "for she is in dire need." The war had finally reached Sergeant Roncalli.

It seemed that the Lord answered Italy's prayers. On October 24, 1918, the first anniversary of their worst defeat, the Italian army counterattacked and drove the Austrians out of Italy. "The victory of our

Father Roncalli (second row, center) as a teacher of theology at the diocesen seminary in Bergamo in 1919. Roncalli was devoted to teaching as "the formation of the new generation in Christ's spirit." He was called away in 1921 to head the Vatican's Society for the Propagation of the Faith.

AP/WIDE WORLD

UPI/BETTMANN NEWSPHOTOS

arms has been truly grandiose," Roncalli wrote in his journal. This was the last major battle of the war, which ended on November 11, as abruptly as it had begun four years earlier. Italy joined the other victorious allies in the peace talks. His services no longer needed, the recently promoted Lieutenant Roncalli was demobilized on December 10, and he bid farewell to army life. After a three-and-one-half-year diversion, he could return to his priestly career.

The postwar years were a period of hope and optimism for Father Roncalli. He established a youth center for the students attending Bergamo University; he served as chaplain to the Union of Catholic Women, an important local organization; and he

Pope Benedict XV in 1918 distributing food to Italian prisoners of war held by the Germans in Bavaria. As a friend of Bishop Radini Tedeschi, Benedict XV remembered Roncalli, and elevated him to his first important post in the Vatican.

23

was the spiritual director to the students at the Bergamo seminary. There is no question that Roncalli enjoyed his work, but at the age of 37 he was dissatisfied with his career, which seemed to hold little for the future.

Luckily, a seed Roncalli had planted earlier began to show promise. He had written a brief biography of his mentor, Bishop Radini Tedeschi, and the book had fallen into the hands of Cardinal William van Rossen, the head of the Vatican department of foreign missions. Impressed with the book and with Roncalli's record of service in Bergamo, van Rossen wrote to Roncalli and asked him to come to the Vatican to serve as the Italian director of the Society for the Propagation of the Faith, the Church's major foreign mission organization. Although Roncalli had some doubts about serving in such a formidable position, he accepted the new assignment.

Roncalli began his new job in January 1921 and he was quickly caught up in the bureaucracy. "This sudden change in the direction of my career has left me astonished and terrified," he wrote in his journal. Yet he was very successful in this new position, more than doubling donations to the society in less than two years. Politically cautious, Roncalli was careful to attribute his success to the work of his superiors.

While traveling throughout the country on mission work, Father Roncalli could not help but notice the rising popularity of the Fascists, a right-wing, doctrinaire political movement. Led by the charismatic Benito Mussolini, the Fascists were popular enough by October 1922 to seize control of the Italian government. Once anticlerical, Mussolini and the Fascists made peace with the Vatican and gained for his government the tacit support of the Church. He would rule Italy as a dictator for the next two decades.

Vatican support for Mussolini did not rest easy with Roncalli. He wrote to his family in April 1924, "His aims may be good and honest, but the means he employs are wicked and contrary to the laws of the Gospel." Roncalli would not have to tolerate Mussolini's rule much longer. Yet another unex-

Mussolini . . . a gift of Providence, a man free from the prejudices of the politicians of the liberal school.

—POPE PIUS XI
on the Italian dictator
Benito Mussolini

pected shift in his career would take him away from Italy for the next two decades.

During the first half of his life Angelo Roncalli had had many occupations. As a student, priest, soldier, and bureaucrat he had learned lessons that would be valuable to him in later life. Yet Angelo Roncalli felt ill-prepared for his next assignment. On February 17, 1925, Father Roncalli was informed that Pope Pius XI had appointed him "apostolic visitor" to the eastern European nation of Bulgaria.

The Fascists, led by Benito Mussolini, march on Rome in November 1922. The Vatican entered into an uneasy alliance with Mussolini, which finally led to the creation of Vatican City as a sovereign state in 1929. Roncalli was uneasy about the Vatican's dealings with Mussolini, whose actions he thought "contrary to the laws of the Gospel."

2

A Mission in the East

*He is a most lovable person,
and it is owing to his
natural goodness of soul that
a large part of his success
as a diplomat is due.*
—CARDINAL MONTINI
archbishop of Milan

Angelo Roncalli was an unlikely candidate to become a Vatican diplomat. He was a short, rotund, diocesan priest of humble background. He spoke no languages other than Latin and his native Italian. He had left his homeland only a few times before, to visit religious shrines in France and Palestine, and for a two-week tour of western Europe in 1921–22. To be sure, he had distinguished himself as a fund-raiser for the missions, but that was not a skill used in the elite Vatican diplomatic corps.

Roncalli was very surprised, therefore, when he learned that the pope had selected him for a politically sensitive diplomatic mission in, of all places, Bulgaria. His assignment was to visit that country, provide strength and encouragement to the small Catholic community there, and report back to the Vatican on the state of Bulgarian Catholicism. To add prestige to his appointment as an apostolic visitor, he was to be elevated from the rank of priest to archbishop. "Why me," Roncalli asked, since he had sought neither the assignment nor the promotion. There was no answer to this question. The reason for the assignment remained with the pope. It was this minor bit of mystery that launched An-

THE BETTMANN ARCHIVE

Ferdinand I was the first king of modern Bulgaria. When Austria-Hungary annexed part of the Ottoman lands in the Balkans in 1908, Ferdinand seized the opportunity to declare Bulgaria's independence. Ten years later he was forced to abdicate in favor of his son, Boris III, after fighting on the losing side in World War I.

Father Roncalli visiting his home in Sotto il Monte in 1921. Roncalli had been noticed by the Vatican for his biography of Bishop Radini Tedeschi, and his works of hagiography (writings on saints' lives). Soon he would be assigned to the elite Vatican diplomatic corps.

gelo Roncalli on a 20-year mission in eastern Europe and the Middle East.

Roncalli had received a difficult assignment for a novice diplomat. Bulgaria was a country in the midst of chaos in 1925. For many years it had been a part of the Ottoman Empire, a vast territory that stretched from the Middle East to eastern Europe around the eastern edge of the Mediterranean Sea. For hundreds of years this empire had been ruled by the Turks. But in 1908, under the leadership of King Ferdinand, the Bulgarians defeated the Turks and finally achieved their independence.

It was a nation in name only. Though united in their struggle against the Ottoman Empire, the many different ethnic and religious groups in Bulgaria began fighting among themselves after independence. Tensions led to violence and frequent efforts to kill the king and overthrow the government. "Everyone seems to be fighting everyone else," Roncalli was told before he left the Vatican.

This fact was dramatically clear to Roncalli on April 25 as he stepped off the train in Sofia, the capital of Bulgaria. The city was in an uproar. King Boris III, who had succeeded his father as the leader of Bulgaria, had survived two assassination attempts in the previous two weeks. In the second attack, the foreign minister and several hundred people had been killed.

The archbishop had an uncertain diplomatic status in Bulgaria. He was the first papal representative in the country in over five centuries, but he had no official relations with the Bulgarian government. Roncalli was, as his title stated, only a visitor. Making matters more difficult for him was the fact that he had never received a specific set of instructions from the Vatican regarding his mission. Apparently, he was free to address problems as he saw fit. "May my mission be one of reconciliation in words and deeds," he wrote at the time of his appointment. Roncalli worked hard to make it so.

The first problems he addressed were pastoral — to build a bridge between the two factions of the Catholic church in Bulgaria. Even though Catholics constituted less than one percent of the Bulgarian

> *Wherever I may go in the world, anyone from Bulgaria who might be in distress and who comes by my house at night will find a light in my window. Knock, just knock, and I shall not ask you whether you be Catholic or Orthodox, just knock and enter, brother Bulgarians!*
> —JOHN XXIII
> as apostolic visitor
> to Bulgaria

population, they were divided into Latin Catholics, who used a liturgy common in Western nations, and Uniate Catholics, who had a liturgy that incorporated many Eastern religious customs. There was little communication between the 48,000 Latin Catholics and 12,000 Uniate Catholics in the country in 1925.

The archbishop devoted the first few months of his mission to a tour of the many rural villages of Latins and Uniates scattered across the desolate country. Traveling mostly by horse or oxcart, his visits became important events for these settlements. Small children would run through the streets announcing the arrival of "Diado" — the "good father." His willingness to reach out endeared him to these rural Catholics, and the feeling of affection was mutual. "Believe me," he wrote to a friend many years later, "when I remember those dear people, my heart is moved and my eyes are filled

The second wedding of Boris III of Bulgaria to Princess Giovanna of Italy in the Orthodox Alexander Nevsky Cathedral, November 11, 1930. The couple had already married two weeks earlier in a Roman Catholic ceremony.

Archbishop Roncalli in 1936, as apostolic delegate to Turkey and Greece. Roncalli's strong belief in ecumenism — the promotion of unity and cooperation among people of all faiths — had begun in Bulgaria and continued in Turkey where the archbishop tried to bring unity to the Catholic factions and to restore good relations between the Catholic minority and the Orthodox church.

with tears." Both the Latins and the Uniates came to trust Roncalli and through him to communicate with each other.

Roncalli also devoted time to building bridges with other religious denominations in Bulgaria. The vast majority of the country was Orthodox, a Christian denomination that had resulted from a schism within the Catholic church in the year 1054. In fact, Orthodoxy was the state religion in Bulgaria and had bonded the nation together during its struggle for independence.

Even though the Orthodox had many of the same religious traditions as the Catholics, there was distrust and hostility between the two faiths. The arrival of an apostolic visitor from Rome, therefore, was viewed with suspicion. Many Orthodox churchmen thought that Roncalli was in Bulgaria on an evil mission to bring the nation back into communion with Rome.

Roncalli did not take these groundless charges personally. Quietly he worked to open communication between himself and the leaders of the Orthodox church in Bulgaria. Finally in March 1927 he was able to meet with the patriarch, the head of the church, and work toward a state of mutual trust and respect. It was a small but important sign of Roncalli's later contributions as an ecumenist.

After two years in Bulgaria, however, Roncalli's spirit began to wane. At the time of his assignment he had been told that he would be in Bulgaria for only a few months and then reassigned to a Latin American country. But months extended into years. Making matters worse, Roncalli's suggestions for improvements in the Bulgarian Catholic church were largely ignored at the Vatican. "My ministry has brought me many trials," he wrote in his journal in December 1926, "but these are not caused by the Bulgarians for whom I work, but by the [Vatican]. This is a form of mortification and humiliation that I did not expect and which hurts me deeply." Roncalli began to feel that the Vatican really did not care about Bulgarian Catholicism.

This may have been the case, but an incident in October 1929 forced the Vatican to take notice of

Roncalli and the Bulgarian Catholic church. King Boris III of Bulgaria proposed to marry Princess Giovanna of Italy. Because the bride was a Catholic and because the couple was to be married in a Catholic ceremony, Boris and Giovanna sought the permission of Church officials to get married. The king assured Roncalli that the sole marriage ceremony would be Catholic and the children would be raised as Catholics. With these assurances, the marriage was solemnized in a Catholic wedding mass at Assisi in Italy.

But Boris did not keep his promise. After the couple triumphantly returned to Sofia, King Boris agreed to a second marriage ceremony in the Orthodox cathedral. It is likely that his motivation was political. Simply put, Boris could not rule Bulgaria if he did not profess the Orthodox faith.

The pope was furious at this turn of events. He lashed out at Boris in a papal message on Christian marriage. For his part in the affair, Roncalli earned a reputation for being naive and foolish. Many Vatican officials thought he should never have trusted the king. Roncalli was sure that he would be recalled to Rome in disgrace, but it never happened. Perhaps the pope believed that a few more years in Bulgaria was the best punishment for this trusting diplomat.

Roncalli would spend another five years in Bulgaria. His letters home and his journal show a steady decline in his spirit. Life in Bulgaria was a major cause of his depression. He was further depressed by the news that King Boris and Queen Giovanna would not honor their commitment to raise their children in the Catholic faith. The children would be raised Orthodox. "The prolongation of my life in this country," he wrote in his journal, "often brings me severe personal suffering which I force myself to hide."

Roncalli's Bulgarian exile came to an end in December 1934. He received a cable from the Vatican shortly before Christmas. As soon as possible he was to travel to Istanbul, the largest city in Turkey, to take up new duties as apostolic delegate. He was to be the pope's representative to the Catholics of that country. He would not be formally acknowledged as

> *My brethren, my sons! You who feel the weight of grief, you whose shoulders bend under the load of human misery, you whose soul is sorry with the uncertain vision of the future, let me inspire you with courage, let me comfort you from the first moment of my meeting with you.*
> —JOHN XXIII
> upon his arrival in Turkey

a diplomat by the Turkish government, but he had to be sensitive to the politics of the country. The previous delegate had alienated both the Catholic community and the Turkish government. A peace-maker was needed, and the pope thought that Roncalli was just the man for the job.

There was no lack of work to do. The number of Catholics in Turkey was larger than in Bulgaria, and the community was even more divided. In addition to Latins and Uniates, there were also Melkite, Armenian, Greek, and Chaldean Catholics to contend with. All of these groups had distinct religious traditions that divided them from one another. Roncalli also faced hostility from the Turkish government, which was suspicious of all religious leaders in the nation.

As if these burdens were not enough, Roncalli was given additional responsibility for the Catholics of Greece, a community fraught with even greater problems than those of Turkey. "What more do I need by way of opportunities," he wrote in his journal, "to make myself holy?"

The archbishop faced the same three tasks in Turkey and Greece that he had faced in Bulgaria. He had to be a pastor, an ecumenist, and a diplomat. As a pastor, he worked to unify the Turkish Catholic community by reminding the various factions that they were all equal in the eyes of God and the pope. "All people were invited equally to sit down at the same banquet of heavenly doctrine," he preached, "and share in the grace that sanctifies and rejoices the heart." As part of his pastoral ministry, Roncalli learned the languages and liturgical rituals of these various groups. In doing so, he earned the respect of all segments of the Turkish Catholic community.

As an ecumenist, he worked with what he called "the outer circles of humanity" — a nearer circle of non-Catholic Christians and a farther circle of non-Christians and nonbelievers. His ecumenical achievements were symbolized in the presence of a representative of the Orthodox church at a Catholic liturgy celebrating the election of Pope Pius XII in March 1939. In a later meeting with the patriarch, the spiritual head of the Orthodox church, Ron-

> *He who prays is a coward or in any case a useless being.*
> —attributed to Mustafa Kemal (Atatürk), president of Turkey

calli extended the "kiss of peace," yet another important symbol of ecumenism. Roncalli knew that these were small achievements and that he could not single-handedly break down the walls between Christian denominations. "But," said Roncalli, "I try to pull out a brick or two."

As a diplomat, Roncalli faced his most substantial challenges, a consequence of the political climate in Turkey and throughout the world. In the 1930s Turkey was led by Mustafa Kemal, a nationalist who took the name "Atatürk," meaning "father of all Turks." Atatürk opposed all religious denominations because he believed that religious leaders were a threat to his iron-handed rule. To limit the influence of the clergy, Atatürk forbade clerical dress in

Mustafa Kemal (left), known as Atatürk (Father of the Turks), founded the Republic of Turkey after driving out the Sultanate in 1922. As dictator he attempted to modernize Turkey, and though his state was officially Muslim, he opposed *all* religion as a hindrance to progress.

public and he restricted the movement of all religious leaders. When Roncalli traveled from Istanbul to the capital city of Ankara, he did so in a business suit and under police escort.

Roncalli was irritated by these restrictions, but he did not openly oppose them. And he did not allow these restrictions to prevent him from establishing ties with the lower ranks of the Turkish government and with the British, American, French, German, Dutch, Belgian, Polish, and Italian embassies. Roncalli did not achieve much during the 1930s as a result of these contacts. But this groundwork proved invaluable a few years later when the world was consumed by war.

On September 1, 1939, Germany invaded Poland and plunged Europe into a conflict known today as

World War II. Although Turkey was thousands of miles away from the fighting and remained neutral for most of the war, the country was an important listening post for the exchange of information. All of the combative nations had embassies in Turkey, and all of the ambassadors talked on occasion with Roncalli. Because of these communications, the archbishop learned a great deal about war plans and intentions, and he passed this information on to the Vatican.

These communications, however, did little good for Roncalli's reputation as a diplomat. During 1940 Roncalli had regular meetings with the German ambassador, who tried to convince the archbishop that the Germans were seriously interested in world peace, and that Adolf Hitler, the leader of the Ger-

Nazi troops in Poland rounding up women and children. Archbishop Roncalli became involved in plans to transport Jews and other refugees to safe areas when news of their brutal treatment by the Nazis began to spread.

Map of Europe in 1941, showing the conquests of the
Axis forces. After Greece fell to the Germans in April
1941, the Allies blockaded the country, causing famine.
Archbishop Roncalli negotiated with both sides to allow
desperately needed food to cross the blockade.

man government, was a reasonable man. Roncalli conveyed this information to the Vatican without comment. The end result was that Roncalli reinforced his reputation in Rome for being too gullible to be an effective diplomat.

But the Vatican was too quick to dismiss the diplomatic skills of their man in Istanbul. Roncalli's quiet diplomacy allowed him to serve as a key participant in a number of wartime humanitarian efforts. In Greece, in the bitter famine winter of 1941, Roncalli negotiated with the Allies to temporarily lift a blockade of the country so that food supplies could reach the starving civilian population. In 1943 and 1944, the archbishop devoted himself to saving the refugees of war, particularly the Jews.

Between 1933 and 1945, nearly 12 million innocent men, women, and children lost their lives. Many of these people were killed simply because they were Jewish.

The systematic destruction of the Jews, now known as the Holocaust, began in the 1930s in Germany. Led by Hitler, many Germans blamed the Jews for their defeat in World War I and for the worldwide economic depression of that decade. The fact that there was no truth to these charges did not seem to matter. Through the use of slave labor, firing squads, and gas chambers, the Nazis attempted to eliminate the Jewish population. Jews were isolated and sent to concentration camps in Germany, Poland, and other nations — camps with names such as Dachau, Auschwitz, Buchenwald, and Bergen-Belsen.

As a diplomat, Roncalli had heard rumors about the Holocaust. Yet, communication during the war was poor and the stories, he thought, were too incredible to be true.

But Roncalli learned much more in a meeting with Chaim Barlas of the Jerusalem Jewish Agency. Barlas represented an agency that devoted its energy and resources to helping Jews emigrate to Palestine. But the agency could do little in the face of Hitler's slaughter. Desperate for help, Barlas provided Roncalli with details of the genocide and asked the archbishop to appeal to the pope for help. Would the

> *And what answer do you give me regarding the two and a half million Polish Jews that you are exterminating?*
> —JOHN XXIII
> questioning German Ambassador von Papen on Nazi atrocities in 1941

Catholic church assist Jews in reaching Palestine or some other safe haven? Roncalli agreed to support this humanitarian proposal.

Supporting this appeal was not a simple decision for Roncalli. The pope at the time, Pius XII, feared that if he criticized Nazi Germany, Hitler would attack Catholics and Catholic churches in Europe. All the papal diplomats, including Roncalli, were instructed to follow a policy of strict neutrality toward the warring nations.

It is not surprising, therefore, that Roncalli's appeal was not warmly received in Rome. Papal officials claimed that they had already asked neutral nations to accept Jewish refugees with little result. In spite of new evidence of massive killing, they saw no reason to appeal a second time.

It was a diplomatic response to a humanitarian plea. Roncalli had been rebuffed, but not defeated. He could not forget the information from Chaim Barlas. In spite of the pope's neutrality, and the risk of offending the German government, the archbishop joined the campaign to save Jewish lives.

Germans in the 1920s trade potato peels for wood. The harsh peace terms after World War I had contributed to skyrocketing inflation in Germany: the mark fell to 4 trillion to the dollar. This helped lead to the rise of Nazism and World War II.

During the spring and summer of 1943 Roncalli worked with King Boris of Bulgaria to help save the lives of more than 24,000 Jews in that nation. These refugees were fleeing the German army and were in immediate danger of being sent to the death camps. In order to help the Jews leave Bulgaria quickly, Roncalli provided them with special transit visas to Palestine. The plan succeeded and even papal officials came to appreciate the archbishop's practical humanitarianism.

The success of the first Bulgarian operation encouraged Roncalli to try it a second time. King Boris was the key man; he made the escape possible by insuring that the visas got into Jewish hands. The archbishop understood this and tried to motivate his friend. In June, Roncalli wrote Boris, encouraging him to continue his efforts to save Jewish

Adolf Hitler salutes his soldiers in Vienna in March 1938, two weeks after the Germans occupied Austria. The Vatican followed a policy of neutrality during World War II, which lost the Catholic church prestige when the war was over.

lives. In response the king said that he would do what he could, adding that the Nazis had limited his authority. This letter to Roncalli was among the king's last. Boris died mysteriously, returning from a trip to see Hitler. Roncalli had lost both a close friend and a valuable ally.

In the early months of 1944, Roncalli focused his attention on a second group of refugees. This time it was Jews trapped in Romania. In February, he met with Isaac Herzog, the chief rabbi of Jerusalem, to discuss the fate of 55,000 Jews living in a desolate region of that country. If they were not moved soon, the Germans would kill them.

There was little time, so Roncalli worked swiftly to convince papal officials to intercede with the Romanian government. By the end of March the Romanians had agreed to release the Jews, and Roncalli and Herzog were optimistic that the refugees would soon be out of danger. The chief rabbi was grateful. "The people of Israel," Herzog wrote to Roncalli, "will never forget the help brought to its unfortunate brothers and sisters . . . at this, the

saddest moment in our history."

But papal intervention alone would not be enough to protect these and other Jews from the German army. The pope had no influence with Hitler and it was only a matter of time before the army located the remaining Jews and transported them to the concentration camps.

With time running out, Roncalli became frustrated at his inability to do more. He could provide transit visas, but who would provide the ships and the trains to transport the refugees to safety? By the end of March more than 7,000 Jews were ready for transport out of Romania. Government officials were ready to release them, but would not provide transportation. The archbishop had no ships or trains at his disposal, so many of the Jews were unable to escape. This was the dilemma that Roncalli faced.

The transportation problem continued throughout the summer of 1944. Arrangements with the Romanian government to release its Jews bogged down for lack of ships. In July the archbishop re-

The German army and the Hitler Youth marching in the streets. The Nazis militarized the German youth as part of Hitler's plan for a thousand years of German rule in Europe.

King Boris III of Bulgaria. In 1943 Boris worked with Archbishop Roncalli to transport Jews out of Bulgaria before they were rounded up by the Germans. Boris died mysteriously on August 28, 1943, following a heated interview with Adolf Hitler.

UPI/BETTMANN NEWSPHOTOS

ported the arrival in Istanbul of a ship with a mere 730 refugees, far short of the 55,000 that Roncalli had hoped to save.

Frustrated by the lack of progress, and fearful of the actions of the German army, Roncalli sent thousands of immigration certificates into Hungary and Romania. Prepared by Chaim Barlas and the staff of the Jerusalem Jewish Agency, these certificates conferred no real rights, but they did afford some protection.

Perhaps the most interesting aspect of this frenzied distribution plan is a rumor that emerged after the war. It was widely quoted that Roncalli had distributed baptismal certificates to the Jews. Such a rash course of action would have been out of character for a papal diplomat such as Roncalli. To be sure, some Catholic priests did use baptismal certificates to protect the Jews, but not Roncalli. He distributed only immigration certificates.

As the war worsened, Roncalli found it impossible to get even the immigration certificates into eastern Europe. On August 2, 1944, Turkey abandoned its neutrality and broke relations with Germany. With this act, Roncalli was forced to become a bystander in the campaign to save the Jews.

Roncalli's efforts to save Jewish lives were significant acts of humanitarianism, but they should be kept in historical perspective. Roncalli was not a hero who took great personal risks, he was a diplomat who did what he could to help his fellow man. Many other Catholics risked a great deal to save the lives of Jews. When put in this context, Roncalli played only a small part in the worldwide campaign against the Holocaust.

What makes Roncalli's Holocaust experience important is its lasting impact on his beliefs, and the effect of those beliefs on Catholic thought. As a Christian, Roncalli believed that Christ had died to proclaim universal brotherhood among people of all faiths. The Holocaust symbolized for him the despicable results of religious hatred. As Pope John XXIII, Roncalli would work to break down the barriers that had existed between Catholics and Jews for centuries. Never again could a nation be allowed to defile Christ's message as the Germans had done in their war against the Jews.

Roncalli best summarized his views on religious brotherhood shortly after becoming pope. "I am your brother," he greeted a group of American Jews. "We are all sons of the same Father. We come from the Father and must return to the Father." It was this deep belief in religious brotherhood and world peace that he shared during his brief tenure as a world leader. It was a gift that many people of all religious faiths came to cherish.

As Christmas 1944 approached, Roncalli looked forward to a new year when there might be peace on earth and goodwill toward men. He was about to begin his 11th year in Turkey and he had no reason to think that his life or his mission would change in 1945. He was shocked, therefore, when he decoded a message from the Vatican ordering him to pack his bags. The cable informed Roncalli that he

Two survivors of the Nazi death camp in Nordhausen, Germany. The discovery of the death camps shocked the world. More than 6 million Jews were murdered in camps like Auschwitz, Bergen-Belsen, Dachau, and this one in Nordhausen, liberated by the Allies on April 11, 1945.

Dr. Isaac Halevy Herzog, chief rabbi of Palestine, was one of the first to raise the alarm about the Holocaust. When Roncalli became pope in 1958, Herzog sent a warm note remembering Roncalli's help in the effort to save Romania's Jews.

was to proceed to Paris to take up duties as papal ambassador to France.

He could not believe what he read. He was a 63-year-old man expecting to retire soon. He had done a mediocre job as a papal representative in two minor nations in the East. He was hardly the logical candidate for the most prestigious post in the Vatican diplomatic corps. As had been the case with his appointment to Bulgaria, there was no clear explanation. It was a personal decision of the pope. Roncalli had no choice but to obey.

As he packed, the archbishop could reflect on almost two decades of service in the East — in the nations of Bulgaria, Turkey, and Greece. He had faced a variety of challenges as a diplomat, as a pastor, and as an ecumenist, and he had struggled to meet those challenges. But, for all his efforts, Roncalli was not much of a diplomat in the conventional sense. He lacked the instinct for strategy that is the sign of an outstanding diplomat. He was too gullible, putting too much faith in his fellow man.

But the Vatican was also aware of Roncalli's abilities as a pastor and an ecumenist. He had done much to heal the wounds within the Catholic communities of Bulgaria, Turkey, and Greece. He had established lines of communication with denominations long out of touch with the Catholic church. These skills had singled Roncalli out from his colleagues. He was, in fact, a logical candidate to help heal the wounds of war-torn France.

Four years of Nazi occupation had left France devastated by the time Roncalli arrived in Paris as papal nuncio, or ambassador. His mission from 1944 until 1952 was to heal the wounds caused by war.

3

Healing Wounds in the West

It was an abrupt and startling transition. After nearly 20 years in Bulgaria, Turkey, and Greece, Angelo Roncalli had accustomed himself to Eastern culture. Now, with little more than a few weeks' notice, he was on his way to Paris, one of the major capitals of Western Europe. He prayed for God's help in his new position as papal ambassador to France.

The challenge of his new assignment was more than evident to Roncalli. He knew that he was traveling to a nation that had been changed utterly by world war. From the spring of 1940 to the summer of 1944, France had been under the control of the German army. Hitler had seized France along with other Western European nations to create an empire he called "fortress Europe."

The surrender of France in the spring of 1940 had been a shock to the French people. In the confusion, the French parliament had agreed to a German plan to divide their country. The northern half of France would be controlled directly by the German army. The southern half would be administered by a German-controlled French government with a capital at the city of Vichy in central France.

AP/WIDE WORLD

Marshal Henri Philippe Pétain. A hero of World War I, Pétain headed the collaborationist Vichy government during World War II, and was condemned as a traitor after the war. He died in prison in 1951.

Papal Nuncio Roncalli greeting a schoolboy in Paris in 1947. Roncalli's arrival in France coincided with a great controversy over bishops who had cooperated with the fallen Vichy government. Roncalli's soothing diplomacy helped restore the tarnished reputation of the Church.

The French people were as divided as their nation. Some collaborated with the German and Vichy governments. Others fought back, joining a secret organization known as "the Resistance." Thousands of men and women who were members of the Resistance were imprisoned, tortured, and killed by the Germans.

The end of "fortress Europe" and the German domination of France came in the summer of 1944. On "D-Day," June 6, 1944, Allied troops landed on the beaches of northern France. The Allies — Great Britain, the United States, Canada, and other nations — pushed the German army back through the countryside of France. In August Paris was liberated, and by the end of September the Germans were out of France entirely.

The war in France had been costly. Hundreds of thousands of French citizens had died for their nation. The new French government led by Charles de Gaulle and Georges Bidault vowed to root out all those Frenchmen who had cooperated with either the German army or the Vichy government. The charge "collaborationist" was a curse, and thousands of Frenchmen were arrested and questioned about their activities during the war. Many of those questioned were later tried and imprisoned.

When Angelo Roncalli arrived in Paris in December 1944, he found that the French Catholic church was caught up in the collaborationist controversy. The government had accused more than two dozen French bishops, including the archbishop of Paris, of collaborating with the enemy. Even Roncalli's predecessor as papal ambassador had been forced out of France because of such a charge. The French government wanted the Vatican to dismiss all of these offending bishops.

Roncalli knew that dismissal was out of the question. The Vatican would not hear of it. These bishops had committed no crimes, and the pope would not accept French interference with his right to appoint and dismiss bishops. Roncalli was instructed by the Vatican to present the pope's position and to seek an acceptable solution.

Roncalli's strategy was to hold discreet meetings

with both government officials and the offending bishops. He succeeded in getting the government to cut its original list in half. Roncalli convinced two of the dozen bishops still on the list to resign, and a third did so of his own accord. For the others Roncalli pleaded patience, and the French government essentially gave up the fight. As a gesture of respect for the French position, Roncalli secured promotions for three archbishops who had opposed the Vichy government. With these promotions, the case of the collaborationist bishops came to a close.

But the resolution of this conflict did not bring peace to French Catholicism. During the war years, the archbishop of Paris had promoted an experiment to bring his priests in closer communication with the working classes. It was a pastoral movement that sent young priests into the factories to work alongside the laity in order to learn more about the spiritual and material needs of the workers. These clergymen were known as "worker priests." By the end of the decade, the movement had swept across France. Many priests saw it as a way of revitalizing French Catholicism.

But the Vatican was suspicious. Through Ron-

American reinforcements land on the beaches at Normandy, France, in June 1944. Operation Overlord was the largest naval invasion force in history, and marked the beginning of the end of the war in Europe.

AP/WIDE WORLD

calli the Vatican asked the archbishop of Paris several questions about the worker-priest experiment. Why this new form of apostolate? Did it not harm the traditional ministry of the priest? Were there no other ways of reaching the workers? The French archbishop replied by defending the movement and implying that Vatican bureaucrats could not understand the alienation of the working classes without experiencing factory life firsthand. For the time being, the Vatican allowed the worker-priest movement to continue.

It is not clear where Roncalli stood on this issue. When asked by the Vatican for his opinion, Roncalli advised that the experiment should be allowed to continue until it was either a clear success or a clear failure. From his comments to the archbishop of Paris and others, it is likely that Roncalli found the worker-priest idea to be intriguing but unsound. Throughout his life Roncalli firmly believed that ordination to the priesthood made a man special in God's eyes, as well as in the eyes of his fellow mortals. A priest would never be accepted as just

Albert Camus, Nobel Prize-winning French writer and intellectual. Camus was the spokesman for a generation disaffected with religion. The Church responded by calling for strict adherence to Catholic doctrine, thus alienating many French Catholics.

UPI/BETTMANN NEWSPHOTOS

another worker. A priest was a priest, Roncalli thought, and that was that.

The worker-priest experiment continued until August 1953, when the Vatican ordered the archbishop of Paris to end it. The pope had run out of patience. The movement had never become the clear success or failure that Roncalli expected. But the formal termination of the experiment did not end the movement. Many of the worker priests refused to leave their factory jobs and some had to be excommunicated from the Church for disobedience. In the end, the termination of the worker-priest experiment left French Catholicism bitterly divided.

The third controversy that Roncalli faced in France involved intellectual freedom. The years after World War II were an intellectual renaissance in France. Philosophers such as Albert Camus and Jean-Paul Sartre questioned the meaning of human existence. Novelists such as François Mauriac and Georges Bernanos wrote movingly of the importance of religious faith in a secular society. Even Catholic theologians began to reinterpret Catholic doctrine in the aftermath of the world war. Priests such as Henri de Lubac, Yves Congar, and Pierre Tielhard de Chardin were among the most prominent of these theologians. It was an exciting time to be in France.

But intellectual speculation, especially on matters of Church doctrine, made the Vatican uneasy. In 1950 the pope issued an encyclical, or papal message, that called for rigid adherence to Catholic doctrine. Many Catholic theologians, most notably Congar and de Lubac, were forbidden to write or publish on theological topics. This was not a popular message in France. The censorship of French Catholic theologians added tension to the already strained relations between the French Catholic church and the Vatican.

Once again Roncalli was the man in the middle of a controversy. He was criticized by some French Catholics for not defending these theologians and by others for not seeking a harsher punishment. But anyone who knew Angelo Roncalli would have expected him to take a middle position. Although

> *I am content, like Abraham, to go forward in the night, one step after another, by the light of the stars.*
> —JOHN XXIII

he was no intellectual himself, he had many friends who were writers and scholars. He also tended to think that the Vatican spent too much time on the fine points of doctrine. Nevertheless, he was always conscious of being the pope's representative in France, and, loyal diplomat that he was, he carried out papal policy without comment. The theologians were to be silenced.

As 1952 came to a close, Roncalli had suffered his way through three major Church controversies in France. How much longer would the pope keep him in Paris? His job as ambassador was to be temporary, but just like his work in Bulgaria and Turkey, it had gone on for years and years. In 1952 Roncalli was nearly 71 years old. He expected to semi-retire as the head of a small archdiocese somewhere in Italy, a job that would allow him to live out his remaining years as the pastor he had always wanted to be.

On November 14 Roncalli received a letter from the Vatican that contained news of his new assignment. Semi-retirement would have to wait. The pope asked him if he would accept the position as archbishop of Venice. It was a very important post, one that normally went to younger men. Would he accept such a demanding assignment? "I prayed and thought about it," Roncalli wrote in his journal, "and answered 'obedience and peace.' A totally unexpected new direction in my life."

No doubt Roncalli was pleased and excited. Venice was one of the largest northern Italian cities, less than 150 miles from the village of Sotto il Monte, where he was born, and the city of Bergamo, where he was educated and began his priestly career. After almost three decades as a papal diplomat he was going home. "It is interesting to note that Providence has brought me back to where I began to exercise my priestly vocation," he wrote, "that is, to pastoral work. Now I am ministering directly to souls."

Roncalli's new assignment was not made public at the time of his acceptance because of an unusual circumstance. The archbishop he was to replace was on his deathbed. Out of respect for this man,

> *I never aspired to be more than a country priest in my own diocese.*
>
> —JOHN XXIII

Roncalli would remain as papal ambassador to France for the next few months. In the meantime, the pope made Roncalli a cardinal, a rank that put him among the pope's select advisers. There were only about 70 cardinals in the world at that time. It was a position of power and prestige that admitted Roncalli into the small group of men who selected new popes.

Finally, in March 1953, after the death of his predecessor, Roncalli traveled to Venice to take up an assignment that he expected to be his last. After all, he was 71 years old; his predecessor had been only 65 at the time of his death. Yet Roncalli was not going to sit around waiting for death and his eternal reward. He would use the time he had left to its best advantage. "For the few years that remain for me to live," he wrote, "I want to be a real pastor in the full sense of the word."

> *Do not look upon your patriarch as a man of politics, as a diplomat. Look for the shepherd of souls.*
> —JOHN XXIII
> from his first address as archbishop and patriarch of Venice

AP/WIDE WORLD

Cardinal Roncalli as the newly installed archbishop of Venice in January 1953. Roncalli was 71 and expecting to retire when he received the assignment, but he was excited to return to his home in northern Italy, in the same region as Bergamo and Sotto il Monte.

This was the theme of his first address to his new archdiocese. "The position entrusted me in Venice is a great one," he said to his flock, "It is beyond my merits. But I would ask you to be indulgent to a man who wants simply to be your brother, loving, approachable, understanding." There, on the steps of St. Mark's Cathedral, he embraced the city of Venice as its new pastor.

His years in Venice were relatively quiet compared to his years as a diplomat. Yet these were also years of both joy and sorrow. On the one hand he found great happiness in ministering directly to the people. On the other hand he was frustrated because his financial resources were limited while the demand for assistance was large.

He shouldered his burden quite willingly. If his resources would not suffice to feed all of the needy, he would find more money. His love for the Venetian

Pope Pius XII and Cardinal Roncalli in the Vatican in March 1958. Pius XII had appointed Roncalli ambassador to Paris, and later cardinal, the highest rank in the Church under the pope.

AP/WIDE WORLD

people was evident in his correspondence. "I am content," he wrote of his life in Venice, "because it really gives me great joy. I do not need to use harsh means to keep good order. Watchful kindness, patience, and forbearance get me along much further and more quickly than severity and the rod." Roncalli could have asked for no better assignment to end his years of service to the Church.

But Roncalli's peaceful sojourn as a pastor in Venice came to an end in October 1958. After almost 20 years as pope of the Roman Catholic church, Pius XII died at his summer home outside of Rome on October 9. Who would be the next pope? This question was very much on the mind of Angelo Roncalli, for he would soon travel to the Vatican to join his fellow cardinals in the selection. He prayed to the Lord for guidance.

Roncalli said these prayers with some trepidation. There was a good chance that he would be the next pope; his years of service in both the East and the West made him a logical candidate. He knew that this would be an extraordinary honor — the opportunity to shape the future of the Catholic church. But as he approached his 77th birthday, he was not sure that he had the energy for such a demanding job. Roncalli vowed not to do anything to influence his fellow cardinals. If Angelo Roncalli was to be pope, it would be the Lord's will.

A crowd waits to view the body of Pius XII in front of Castel Gandolfo, where Pius died October 9, 1958. Catholic law states that within 20 days of a pope's death the cardinals must convene to elect a new pope.

L'OSSERVATORE ROMANO

GIORNALE QUOTIDIANO ☩ POLITICO RELIGIOSO

UNICUIQUE SUUM · NON PRAEVALEBUNT

A. XCVIII · N. 252 (29.917)   CITTA DEL VATICANO   Mercoledì 29 Ottobre 1958

ANNUNTIO VOBIS GAUDIUM MAGNUM
HABEMUS PAPAM
EMINENTISSIMUM AC REVERENDISSIMUM DOMINUM CARDINALEM

ANGELO GIUSEPPE RONCALLI

QUI SIBI NOMEN IMPOSUIT

IOHANNES XXIII

Come Pietro:

«Pastor et nauta»

FOTO GIORDANI

4

A Shepherd Called John

If I see a cross before me, I know that I must follow it to the end of the road, even to crucifixion.
—JOHN XXIII

There was no shortage of possible successors to Pope Pius XII. By tradition the cardinals would meet in Rome to select the new pope from among themselves. Some of them supported Cardinal Alfredo Ottaviani, head of the Vatican department concerned with Church doctrine. Others suggested that the new pope should be Cardinal Peter Agagianian, head of the Vatican department concerned with missionary work. A third name put forward was that of Cardinal Angelo Roncalli, the archbishop of Venice. In addition to these three, the names of half a dozen other cardinals were mentioned from time to time. All of these cardinals had served well during many years, but which one would make the best pope?

The Vatican buzzed with speculation. A good part of the talk focused on the qualities that the cardinals should look for in a future pope. Should it be a man who promised continuity, or should he be someone who advocated change? Should the new pope be a young man who could lead the Church for several decades, or should it be an older man who would rule a short time while a younger car-

AP/WIDE WORLD

Cardinal Gregory Agagianian, leader of the Armenian Catholics. Although activity in the conclave, or assembly of cardinals, is secret, it is known that Agagianian and Roncalli were the principal choices for the papacy. On the 11th ballot, the election was decided in favor of Roncalli.

L'Osservatore Romano announces the election of Pope John XXIII, October 29, 1958. Articles in the Vatican City newspaper are written in a variety of languages, the most important Church news appearing in Latin. The headline calls John XXIII *"Pastor et Nauta,"* Latin for "shepherd and helmsman."

UPI/BETTMANN NEWSPHOTOS

dinal was groomed for the job? It seemed that everyone had a favorite candidate, but no one knew how the cardinals would vote.

To insure that the cardinals' deliberations would remain secret, no one would be allowed in or out of the Vatican palace until a new pope was elected. Just before entering the palace the cardinals listened carefully to Cardinal Antonio Bacci, who had been selected to deliver a sermon on the qualities that he and his colleagues should look for in a new pope. "We need a new pope gifted with great spiritual strength and ardent charity," noted Bacci. "May the new vicar of Christ form a bridge between all levels of society, between all nations — even those that reject the Christian religion." This was a large order. The cardinals looked at one another and wondered if such a man was among them. On

Two priests read prayer books outside of St. Peter's while waiting for the announcement of a new pope. White smoke from a Vatican chimney announces to Rome that a new pope has been elected, followed by the traditional announcement "Habemus papam" — "We have a pope."

October 25 the cardinals marched in formal procession into the Vatican palace.

Details of the conclave are very sketchy because the cardinals remained true to their vow of secrecy. From what is known, it is clear that the election was a tight contest between only two men: Cardinals Agagianian and Roncalli. For the first two days of voting, the cardinals could not decide which of these men should be pope. One cardinal reportedly said that "the names of Roncalli and Agagianian went up and down like two chick peas in boiling water." A two-thirds majority of those voting was necessary for one of the two cardinals to be elected. Ballot after ballot proved inconclusive.

As the conclave extended into its third day, however, Roncalli began to gain votes. Because he was well known and well liked in both Eastern and West-

ern countries, Roncalli received many votes on every ballot, enough to block Agagianian or anyone else from obtaining a two-thirds majority. When it was clear to those opposing Roncalli that he was the only viable candidate, he began to receive additional votes. Finally, on the 11th ballot, Angelo Roncalli was elected head of the Roman Catholic church.

After the balloting, Cardinal Eugene Tisserant, the senior cardinal present, turned to Roncalli and asked "Do you accept?" Roncalli answered, "Seeing the signs of God's will in the votes of my brother cardinals of the Holy Roman church, I accept the decision they have made; I bow my head before the cup of bitterness and my shoulders before the yoke of the cross." With these words, Angelo Roncalli became pope.

The answer to the next question was something of a surprise. "By what name do you wish to be known?" asked Tisserant. "I will be called John," responded Roncalli. A murmur went through the assembled cardinals. There had not been a pope named John in several hundred years. Pope John would later explain that he chose his new name in honor of his father, the church where he had been baptized, and two great evangelical saints — John the Baptist and John the Evangelist. Many cardinals and other Catholics suspected that he also chose the name to symbolically break with the policies of his immediate predecessors, most of whom had been named Pius.

That John would be a shrewd leader was evident from the very beginning. His first act as pope was to ask the cardinals to remain in conclave for an additional day to consult with him about the future of the Church. John wanted to draw these men into the decision-making process. Unlike his predecessors, particularly Pius XII, John believed that sharing power would give him greater authority and credibility as both a church and a world leader.

John was also quick to calm the fears of other factions within the Church. Within days of his election, he met with the heads of the various Vatican departments and reappointed them to their positions. There would be no immediate change in the

I shall be called John, a name that is sweet to us because it once was the name of our father, a name which is dear to us because it is the name of the humble parish in which we received our baptism.

—JOHN XXIII
October 28, 1958

Vatican bureaucracy. He spoke with a serenity that calmed even the most apprehensive members of the Church.

This did not mean that John would be the caretaker pope that many had hoped for. John believed that his brother cardinals had given him a mandate for change and he would do everything in his power to implement that change. Indeed, in the first three years of his papacy, the Church would be changed in ways unimaginable to the cardinals who had elected him.

Pope John was comfortable with his new responsibilities. His confidence was a direct result of his deep religious belief that God had personally selected him to serve as pope and that God would direct him in his actions. Because he was God's instrument, John did not fear making the wrong decision. Whatever he decided would be God's will.

Skeptics may scoff at such an explanation of Pope John's style of leadership. Surely, these skeptics will argue, John was manipulative in dealing with oth-

Angelo is able, now that he is pope, to remember a face he saw among the people when he was only a young priest.
—GIUSEPPE RONCALLI
John XXIII's brother

Cardinal Eugene Tisserant, dean of the College of Cardinals in 1958. The dean is the elected head of the sacred college, and speaks on its behalf in dealing with the pope. Cardinal Tisserant presided over the election of John XXIII and received his acceptance of the papacy.

AP/WIDE WORLD

ers. Surely he had personal ambitions for his papacy. Surely he had doubts about the decisions that he made. All of these statements are true and Pope John's diary reflects his concerns about his failures as a leader. But in general, John was confident that his ideas and actions were inspired by God. Not the pope's will, but the Lord's will be done. It was a philosophy of leadership based on humility, a philosophy not easy to understand in our times.

Unlike his immediate predecessors, who chose to lock themselves away in the Vatican, John thought it was important to be involved in the modern world. He was the first pope in more than a century to travel around Italy, and he was particularly active in visiting the destitute and imprisoned in Rome. He firmly believed that Catholics had a right to see their leader in action.

John was also adept at using the media to gain worldwide attention for the papacy and the Church. Previous popes had been stiff and formal in the presence of the press, but John was friendly and infor-

Pope John XXIII blesses the crowd from the balcony of St. Peter's basilica after his elevation to the papacy. The newly elected pope traditionally greets the crowd with a message, beginning with the words *urbi et orbi*, "To the City (Rome) and the World."

mal. He spoke without notes in a simple direct style, and often joked with journalists. Reporters came to think of the pope as a friend.

John was fond of telling stories about himself that journalists cherished and beamed around the world. In his first weeks as pope he told reporters that he was occasionally kept awake at night by various church matters. "I awoke one night," he said with a twinkle in his eye, "and said to myself: 'I will ask the pope about it.' Then I remembered that I was the pope! So I said to myself: 'Right, I will ask God about it.' " He also told the story of a little Italian boy who said to Pope John that he had not decided whether to be a pope or a policeman. "I would become a policeman if I were you," John replied. "Anyone can be a pope — look at me." Stories such as these helped to build a rapport between John and the world beyond the Vatican. Through the media, millions of individuals — both Catholic and non-Catholic — felt a bond of affection for this simple but dignified man.

John's pastoral message of hope and love was evident in almost everything he said and did during the first three years of his papacy. But his major influence during those years came in the form of an encyclical message entitled "Mater et Magistra" ("Mother and Teacher"). An encyclical message is a personal expression of the pope's opinion on major issues of concern to the Church. Such messages often have an influence on the policies of other world leaders, in particular those in countries with large Catholic populations.

"Mater et Magistra" was Pope John's personal reflections on the role of government in the lives of mankind. In this encyclical, Pope John underscored his desire to break with past papal policy. The popes who had preceded John had supported an extremely conservative social order. Most of these popes had flatly rejected all modern forms of government. Pius IX, pope from 1846 to 1878, had attacked democracy. Popes Leo XIII (1878–1903), Pius XI (1922–39), and Pius XII (1939–58) had been critical of trade unions and other forms of self-government. And all of these had condemned even the mildest

What I well know of my poverty and littleness is enough to bring me to confusion. But seeing in the votes of my brethren, the most eminent cardinals of our Holy Roman church, the sign of the will of God, I accept the election made by them.
—JOHN XXIII
after his election as pope

Clockwise, from top left, Pius IX, Leo XIII, Pius XI, and Pius XII. Most of the popes who preceded John XXIII held extremely conservative views on government, rejecting innovations in social order. John's great encyclical "Mater et Magistra" represented a break with the past and a new receptiveness to progressive ideas.

forms of socialism. They feared that the rise of highly centralized and powerful governments would limit the influence of the Church. Instead these popes supported "Christian monarchy" as the ideal form of government. Such antiquated ideas severely limited the influence of the papacy on the modern world.

"Mater et Magistra," however, was a break with this past. John emphasized that workers had a legitimate right to organize in unions to secure what was rightfully theirs. Also, John stated that democracy and other forms of participatory government were important mechanisms for preserving social order that did not diminish the dignity of mankind. Such ideas coming from a pope were, at the very least, unprecedented.

Unlike his predecessors, John did not condemn the social services provided by modern governments. On the contrary, John argued that government services actually could expand the freedoms enjoyed by most citizens. "State involvement," he wrote "makes it possible for an individual to exercise many of his personal rights . . . such as the right to preserve himself in good health; to secure further education and a more thorough professional training; the right to housing, work, suitable leisure and recreation." In sum, the pope was formally recognizing the benefits of the modern welfare state.

"Mater et Magistra" also acknowledged that the expansion of government services came with certain risks. New laws could easily restrict the rights of individuals. To prevent excesses, John proposed that government-chartered but independent institutions be established to provide all social services. Such corporations would serve as a buffer between the government and the people. The pope also favored the widest possible ownership of land so that farmers would not be the employees of the government or predatory land barons.

John also endorsed forms of government that encouraged the widest possible participation of the citizenry. "A natural consequence of men's dignity," he wrote, "is unquestionably their right to take part in public life." Although he did not recommend a

I am persuaded that your noble faith in the highest human values, as shown during the time of the Nazi atrocities, will guide you in your new and important tasks.
—ISAAC HALEVY HERZOG
grand rabbi of Israel,
congratulating John XXIII
on his election to the papacy

John XXIII during a Christmas visit to the Queen of Heaven Prison in Rome in 1958. The pope traveled a great deal in Rome, even reviving the tradition of visiting prisoners. On one visit, he said to the convicts, "Since you can't come to me, I've come to you."

St. John the Baptist (left) and St. John the Evangelist. John XXIII chose his name in honor of his father, the church where he was baptized, and the two saints shown. He may also have wished to make a break with the preceding popes, most of whom were called Pius.

specific form of government, John seemed to favor a model closely resembling the U.S. Constitution which provides for the separation of powers, universal suffrage, and the transcendence of human rights.

To say that "Mater et Magistra" shocked the world is something of an understatement. The encyclical was front-page news throughout the world, including the Soviet Union. The vast majority of comments were very positive — the Catholic church had finally embraced the modern world. But such revolutionary ideas coming from the pope made many conservative Catholics, particularly those in the Vatican bureaucracy, very nervous.

In August 1961, as the publicity over this encyclical began to subside, Pope John reflected back on the first three years of his papacy. He had been criticized in some quarters — particularly within the Vatican — for being too liberal, too quick to abandon Church traditions. John was sensitive to such

Do not be surprised if the pope is a little embarrassed, because many things in the Vatican protocol are new to him.
—JOHN XXIII
to a group of pilgrims
from Bergamo

criticism, yet he had no regrets about the first three years of his papacy. "My conscience is tranquil about my conduct as newly elected pope during these first three years and so my mind is at peace and I beg the Lord always to help me keep faith with these good beginnings."

In August 1961 John was at a transition point in his papacy. "Mater et Magistra" had marked him as a pope of distinction, and he could look back on three very busy years. But John knew well that the years ahead would be even more active. Almost from the day he became pope, John had called for a major council to assess the place of the Church in the modern world. That August, 11 preparatory commissions were busily preparing discussion papers for what was to be the first universal council of the Catholic church in almost a century. John knew even then that the council would be the high point of his papacy. He prayed that he was leading his flock in the right direction.

5

A Universal Council

Our duty is to dedicate ourselves willingly, eagerly, and fearlessly to the work required by our own era, thus proceeding on the way the Church has followed for 20 centuries.
—JOHN XXIII
on Vatican II

It was the evening of October 11, 1962. Earlier that day the pope had convened the Second Ecumenical Vatican Council (now known as Vatican II), the first general council of the Roman Catholic church in almost a century. Such councils were an old tradition in Catholicism. All of the Catholic bishops in the world gathered in one city to determine religious doctrine and discuss issues of concern to the church. Previous councils had defined the basic beliefs of Catholicism. Thus there was excitement in the air that October night. How would this new council change the practice of Catholicism? Would these changes be cosmic or cosmetic? No one, not even Pope John, knew for sure.

The excitement and hope of that day had attracted more than half a million people to St. Peter's Square outside the Vatican palace in Rome. There was singing and dancing and shouts of "Papa, Papa!" The crowd wanted Pope John to come out on his balcony and say a few words to them. The ploy worked. As he stood before that massive crowd John must have been reminded of that day four years earlier when he had been elected pope.

"Dear children, dear children, I hear your voices,"

AP/WIDE WORLD

Cardinal Augustin Bea, a powerful figure in the Curia, the main papal administrative office, was John XXIII's choice to head the "Secretariat for Christian Unity," created to include all Christian denominations in Vatican II. Due to Bea's heroic effort, this controversial goal was achieved.

Pope John XXIII being borne through the nave of St. Peter's Church to open the Second Ecumenical Vatican Council, October 11, 1962. All of the bishops and cardinals in the world were gathered in Rome to decide the future direction of the Church.

he shouted to the crowd. He went on to tell them of his hope for the council. "My voice is an isolated one," he concluded, "but it echoes the voice of the whole world. Here in effect, the whole world is represented." John saw the crowd as a symbol of the laity's desire to celebrate their religious faith. The council, he hoped, would give focus and direction to that celebration.

The opening of the council was an extraordinary triumph for Pope John. For nearly three years he had encouraged, prodded, and even chastised the Vatican officials in charge of council preparations. He rejected pleas that a council was not necessary and that more planning time was needed. There would be a council, John stated flatly, because it was an "inspiration from the Lord." It had been a long, hard journey, but now the council was at last a reality.

The idea for the council emerged very early in John's papacy. In fact, there were stories that John began talking about the need for a council even before he was elected pope. Certainly John had the idea in mind during the months of December 1958 and January 1959 when he conducted research in the Vatican archives on past councils. John himself attributed his final decision on the matter to a meeting on January 20 with his secretary of state, Cardinal Domenico Tardini. From that point on, John never had a second thought about the need for a council.

The only way basically in which we can be good Christians is to do good.
—JOHN XXIII

Few others in the Vatican shared his vision. It was reported that Tardini thought that the pope had gone "temporarily mad." And when John raised the idea at a meeting of Vatican cardinals, he was greeted with "an impressive silence." Even the pope's closest aides advised against a council, believing it would be too much work for an old man.

Beyond the Vatican, the reactions of other Church leaders were mixed. Many of these men feared a new council because previous councils had caused more disunity than unity within the Church. How could a transitional pope start a chain of events that could have disastrous consequences? "Pope John has been rash and impulsive," one cardinal told his

friends. "His inexperience and lack of culture brought this to pass."

The concerns of these Church leaders were understandable. Even though John was determined to hold a council, he was very vague on its purpose and agenda. Was this a new council to condemn the errors of the modern world and defend the Church against her enemies? Or was it to reform the liturgy and doctrine of the Church to bring it into conformity with the modern world? John did not say when he announced the council.

The pope had no intentions of dictating the council agenda. His first act was to establish an "ante-preparatory commission" to gather suggestions from the world's bishops and religious orders on what should be discussed at the council. These sug-

John XXIII in his private library records a radio and television speech announcing to the world his goals for Vatican II: "The light of Christ and the light of the Church should bring light to all nations."

gestions were then turned over to 11 "preparatory commissions" for further review. The preparatory commissions were given the responsibility of preparing formal discussion papers that would be the basis for the council's deliberations. Over 800 cardinals, bishops, and theologians served on these preparatory commissions.

Unfortunately, these deliberations took more than three years to complete. Some historians have suggested that the Vatican cardinals who chaired

Vatican II opens with a procession in St. Peter's Square on the morning of October 11, 1962. Although ill, John XXIII insisted on walking in the procession among the bishops. Nearly 3,000 prelates were in attendance for the council.

the preparatory commissions deliberately delayed their work in the hope that the pope would die and his successor would call off the council. If this was their plan, it backfired. By the beginning of 1962, John had lost patience with the preparatory commissions. On February 2 of that year he announced that the council would open the following October.

While the work of the preparatory commissions dragged on throughout 1960 and 1961, the pope was developing his own ideas on the purpose of the

council. For many years John had been concerned about the millions of "brethren" who were separated from the Catholic church, particularly those people who were members of other Christian denominations. His experience in the East was the foundation of his firm belief that the upcoming council should be open to men of all faiths. He became firmly resolved that the council should include official representatives of all the world's other Christian denominations as well as the bishops of his own Church.

John chose to develop this council theme outside the preparatory commissions. He established a special "Secretariat for Christian Unity" so that Protestants would be able "to follow the work of the council and find more readily the way to attain that unity for which Jesus besought His heavenly father." To head this new secretariat, the pope chose the aged but energetic Cardinal Augustin Bea, the former head of a major theological institute in Rome. It would later prove to be an inspired appointment.

Bea began his work in November 1960 and hardly stopped moving until the opening of the council. He

John XXIII receives a Shinto priest from Japan in a private audience in July 1962. The meeting was a historical first, an indication of John's desire to reach out to all people and all nations.

met with representatives of dozens of Christian denominations, extended the pope's best wishes, and invited them to attend the council. Bea's success was evident at the opening of the council. There were official delegations from the Coptic Christians of Egypt, the Syrian Orthodox, the Armenian Orthodox, the Russian Orthodox in exile, and even the Russian Orthodox in the Soviet Union. There were also representatives of the Western denominations — the Anglicans, the Lutherans, the Calvinists, the Congregationalists, the Quakers, and the Disciples of Christ, among others. In all, there were over 100 Protestant observers at the council. It was truly an ecumenical affair, thanks to Cardinal Bea.

While Cardinal Bea was jetting around the world meeting with Protestant leaders, the preparatory commissions were slowly completing their work. Finally, in June 1962, only four months before the council was to begin, the preparatory commissions turned their papers over to a central commission for further evaluation. The task of this central commission was to establish an agenda for the council, evaluate and revise the discussion papers, choose theologians to act as experts at the council, and

establish parliamentary procedures. The final report of the commission would be something of a blueprint for the council. In fact, some historians have called the work of the central commission a "dress rehearsal" for the council.

The pope had been careful in making appointments to the central commission. Every point of view from traditionalist to progressive was represented. Not surprisingly, conflict and controversy abounded at commission meetings. The traditionalists were led by Cardinals Alfredo Ottaviani and Pericle Felici, both heads of major Vatican departments. The progressives were led by Cardinals Bernard Alfrink of the Netherlands and Franz König of Austria. Membership on the commission ranged between these two factions.

There seemed to be no point of agreement between the traditionalists and the progressives. The traditionalists argued that the purpose of the council was "to condemn the gravest errors of our time and reaffirm the principal points of Catholic doctrine." They could see no role for non-Catholics in the proceedings of the council. The progressives argued that the council should be dedicated to reunion and renewal, not condemnation. The participation of non-Catholics in the council should be encouraged, not discouraged. The meetings of the central commission were held in private, but the arguments first presented at these meetings would later be

John XXIII with Cardinal Giovanni Montini. Montini campaigned for the council to seek positive reform, rather than emphasizing divisions. As Paul VI, Montini would govern over most of Vatican II following John XXIII's death.

UPI/BETTMANN NEWSPHOTOS

John XXIII blesses the crowd in St. Peter's Square from the *sedia gestatoria*, the hand-carried papal chair, as Vatican II opens. The pope was very frail, but he had lived to see the ecumenical council become a reality.

played out before the world at the council.

Even though the pope did not attend the meetings of the central commission, he received reports of the conflict. He had hoped that the Lord would resolve the controversies within the commission. When it was clear that the two sides could not find common ground, John took action on his own. The pope sought the advice of cardinals not associated with the central commission. In this quest, he was particularly impressed with the advice of two men: Cardinals Leo Suenens of Belgium and Giovanni Montini of Italy, the future Pope Paul VI.

Suenens and Montini argued persuasively that the council should emphasize "positive rather than punitive reforms" and be a council of "exhortation rather than anathemas." The council was an opportunity to speak to the entire world, to enter a dialogue with history. Suenens and Montini gave focus to John's vague optimism for the council. During the first session of the council these two car-

John XXIII (center) prays with the cardinals during the opening ceremonies. On the pope's left is Cardinal Alfredo Ottaviani, a traditionalist member of the college who unsuccessfully resisted John XXIII's progressive programs.

dinals were considered by many bishops to be the unofficial representatives of the pope. When they spoke, it was as if the pope was speaking.

John firmly resolved that the council would emphasize the positive. He was distressed, therefore, when he read the first of the discussion papers as revised by the central commission. At one meeting with Cardinal Ottaviani the pope picked up a ruler and measured one of the papers. "Seven inches of condemnation and one of praise," he remarked sarcastically. "Is that the way to talk to the modern world?" It was increasingly clear to Ottaviani that this pope did not support the traditionalist cause.

Even though the central commission had not resolved its internal conflicts, the pope would not delay the start of the council. It would open as announced on October 11. By the end of September bishops from around the world were pouring into Rome. There were 1,200 from the Western nations; a full third of those were from Italy. Latin America was represented by more than 500 bishops, followed by Africa with almost 300. There were over 200 bishops from the United States and nearly 100 from the Far East. In all there were almost 2,500 bishops in Rome to participate in the opening session of the council. The modern world had never seen such a religious spectacle!

The council opened with a speech by Pope John. Some historians have said that it was the speech of his life because it summarized his hopes for Catholicism in general and for the council in particular. In this speech, the pope emphasized four major themes. During the first session of the council, the bishops repeatedly returned to these themes.

First and foremost, John emphasized that the council should be a celebration of the Catholic faith. The simple act of gathering the world's bishops together in one place would renew the spirit of the Church.

Second, John chastised the "prophets of misfortune" for their criticism of the council. This council should bring Catholics closer together, not drive them apart. It was a clear and sharp rebuke to Cardinal Ottaviani and traditionalists. John had fully embraced the philosophy of the council set forth by Cardinals Suenens and Montini.

Third, John stated simply what he and the rest of the world expected of the council. "Christians and Catholics of apostolic spirit all the world over expect a leap forward in doctrinal insight," he proclaimed. "But this authentic doctrine has to be studied in the light of the research methods and the language of modern thought. For the substance of the ancient deposit of faith is one thing, the way in which it is presented is another." This last sentence was an invitation to the bishops to revise and renew the interpretation of Catholic doctrine.

Finally, John cautioned the bishops not to be overly concerned with the condemnation of errors in the modern world. There was no question that incidents of immorality and injustice abounded, but John believed that such errors often disappeared as quickly as they emerged. This council was to emphasize the positive.

This speech and a closing address were the limits of John's official involvement in the council. He believed that the bishops, archbishops, and cardinals should be allowed to shape the future of Catholicism without the pope looking over their shoulders. John had done all that he could to set the council in motion. "He had summoned it," notes historian Paul Johnson, "he had opened it, he had given it advice and encouragement, and he would close it. He held himself in reserve to intervene if necessary. But it was the bishops' work, not his." John believed that the Lord would direct the bishops and the work of the council.

If that was the case then the Lord truly worked in mysterious ways. The first session of the council, which ran from October 22 to December 8, 1962, was characterized by confusion and conflict. There, before God and the world, the bishops of the Catholic church argued over the future of their religion. Everyone claimed to represent the pope's views and appealed to John to intervene and establish order in the proceedings. But John refused these invitations. The bishops would have to work out their disagreements on their own.

True greatness lies in simplicity and in the feeling of God in things.
—JOHN XXIII

The first issue to be addressed was Church liturgy, the fundamental form and content of the Catholic Mass, and other Church services. The discussion paper was generally balanced between traditionalist and progressive views, and many bishops expected that the discussion of this paper would allow the council to open on a positive note.

But two points made the progressive bishops angry. First a section on the biblical foundations of the liturgy, present in earlier versions of the discussion paper, had been removed from the final draft by the traditionalists. The progressives wanted the section restored because it was the basis for the very structure of the liturgy. Second, the traditionalists had added a section to the paper giving authority over the liturgy to the Vatican. The progressives argued that this authority more prop-

erly belonged with the bishops in their home dioceses. These two issues opened the debate on the liturgy.

Once the debate began, however, all kinds of changes were discussed. A large number of bishops favored the use of modern languages rather than Latin in the Mass and other Church services. Other bishops suggested that the laity be allowed to receive the Communion host (bread, usually a wafer) either standing or kneeling, and in the hand as well as on the tongue. Yet another group proposed that priests be permitted to concelebrate the Mass, that is to allow two or more priests to conduct a Mass together. There seemed to be no end to the suggestions, all of them coming spontaneously.

The traditionalist bishops were horrified by these proposals. "Are these fathers plotting revolution?" asked Cardinal Ottaviani. The traditionalists argued that the use of modern languages would split the Church, that receiving the Communion host in the hand was disrespectful, and that concelebration would turn the Mass into theater. They argued vigorously, but changed few minds. Because of the large number of suggested changes, the council voted to return the paper to the preparatory commission for a new draft. A revised paper was prepared, and later it passed the council by an overwhelming majority.

If the debate on the liturgy paper had shocked the traditionalists, they were horrified by the discussion of the sources of divine revelation. For centuries the Church had taught that there were two

THE BETTMANN ARCHIVE

Joan of Arc, who claimed to be guided by heavenly voices, and a page from the Gutenberg Bible. The source of divine revelation caused much debate in the council, traditionalists claiming that only the Vatican could speak with divine authority.

distinct sources of revelation — the word of God as revealed in the Bible and the spirit of God as reflected in the traditions of the Catholic church. The first source was one shared with all Christian faiths. But the second source divided Catholics from all other denominations. On November 14 the bishops began their discussion of the proper balance between these two sources of revelation.

The discussion paper had been prepared by the traditionalists and it placed substantial emphasis on the importance of Church traditions. In fact, the paper sustained a view first promulgated at the Council of Trent, four centuries earlier. The paper stated flatly that only the Vatican could speak with authority on matters of faith. It was as if nothing had changed in over four centuries.

When the debate began, the progressives vigorously attacked the paper. "There are not and never have been two sources of revelation," argued Cardinal Achille Lienart of France. "There is only one . . . the word of God, the good news announced by the prophets and revealed by Christ. The word of God is the unique source of revelation." Many bishops seconded this viewpoint. But the most devastating criticism came from the Secretariat for Christian Unity which argued that the paper was harmful to Catholic relations with other denominations. "It does not represent progress," added one bishop, "but retreat."

It was clear after a few days of discussion that a simple majority of bishops wanted to reject the paper, but a two-thirds majority was required for such an action. To break the deadlock, Pope John suspended the rules so that the will of the majority could prevail. The paper was withdrawn and the pope established a new preparatory commission, one balanced between traditionalists and progressives, to prepare a new paper on the sources of divine revelation. Once again the traditionalists had been defeated.

It was easy to predict what would follow. In meeting after meeting from November 23 to December 2, Cardinal Ottaviani and the traditionalists presented discussion papers. In each case the papers were sent back to the preparatory commissions for revisions.

The rejection of these papers brought little satisfaction to the progressives. In fact, there was a general concern among the bishops that the entire first session of the council had been a failure. Everything had been negative. The bishops had indicated what they did not want, but no progress had been made on defining the doctrines that the council did support. There were dozens of papers yet to be presented. Would the next session, scheduled to begin the following September, be a replay of the first? Most bishops dreaded the thought.

Many bishops were distressed because there still was no overall plan for the council. There needed to be a framework for future sessions, a sense of direction for the work to be done. But who would prepare the plan and lead the council? Certainly not Pope John. He expected the bishops to select a leader or leaders from among their ranks. This was the major problem that vexed the bishops as they prepared for the ceremonies closing the first session of the council on December 8.

But the bishops need not have been concerned. Both the plan and the leader were on the edge of the stage, ready to step forward. On December 2 a dark-eyed cardinal spoke to the assembled bishops about the council and the future. "Some are afraid that the concilar discussions will be endless and that instead of bringing people together it will divide them even more," noted Giovanni Montini. "But that will not happen. The first session has been a training period. The second will progress much more swiftly, and there is already talk of concentrating the material in much briefer drafts and of laying before the council only matters that are justified either by today's pastoral needs or by general interest."

Although he did not give details at that meeting, Montini had a carefully prepared plan for the future sessions of the council. The next session would focus on the nature of the Church and its doctrine. The third session would focus on the mission of the Church and its liturgy. The final session would ad-

> *I come from humble beginnings, and I was raised in a restraining, blessed poverty whose needs are few and which protects the growth of the highest and noblest virtues, and prepares one for the great ascents of life.*
> —JOHN XXIII

John XXIII closes the first meeting of Vatican II on December 8, 1962. He proudly called the first session "a slow and solemn introduction to the great work of the council." The second session of the council reconvened nine months later under a new pope, Paul VI.

dress ecumenism, the Church's relationship with other religious denominations. Little did Cardinal Montini realize that he would lead the council as the next pope, Paul VI.

All of this was in the future, however. Few bishops were as confident about the council as Cardinal Montini. Yet one man, the pope, did share Montini's confidence. At the closing session John, always the optimist, took the opportunity to console the bishops and remind them of the positive aspects of the first session. "Brothers gathered from afar took time to get to know each other," he said. "They needed to look each other in the eyes, to understand each other's hearts; they needed to describe their own experiences, which reflected differences in most varied situations; they needed time to have thoughtful and useful exchanges on pastoral matters."

Future sessions of the council would prove that John's optimism was justified. Unfortunately, John would not live to see his prophecy come true.

John XXIII waves from a train on a pilgrimage to Assisi, to pray at the tomb of St. Francis, patron of the poor. Already seriously ill, he did not show it to the thousands who came to see him on his journey and receive the blessings of their greatly beloved pope.

6

A Pilgrim of Peace

As head of the Roman Catholic church, Pope John had many titles. At the time of his coronation in 1958, the papal crown was placed on his head with the proclamation: "Know that thou art the father of princes and kings, pontiff of the whole world and vicar of Christ on earth." But John largely rejected these titles. This poor peasant boy from Sotto il Monte did not see himself as a king looking down on his subjects. He saw himself as a shepherd tending his flock. John frequently referred to the biblical parable of the good shepherd as his own job description. He was a man largely without pretense.

Yet there is one other title that must be given to John and it is a title that he would have readily embraced. As the "vicar of Christ on earth," John inherited the responsibility of being a man of peace. If Christ was called the "Prince of Peace," John would be the "pilgrim of peace."

It was a job at which he excelled. To be sure, all of the recent popes had been committed to world peace, but their efforts to mediate conflicts had been dismal failures. Pope Benedict XV had tried to mediate during World War I, but his efforts were rebuffed by both sides. Pope Pius XII spoke out on the futility of war, but remained neutral and inactive during World War II. It was hardly a distinguished record for the modern papacy.

But John took this aspect of his job very seriously.

> *My children, love one another. Love one another because this is the great commandment of the Lord.*
> —JOHN XXIII

John XXIII celebrating Easter Mass in 1961. John felt the Church should always lead in the world struggle for peace, and in 1961 he became involved as a mediator in disputes between the United States and Soviet Union, earning praise as a man of peace and reason.

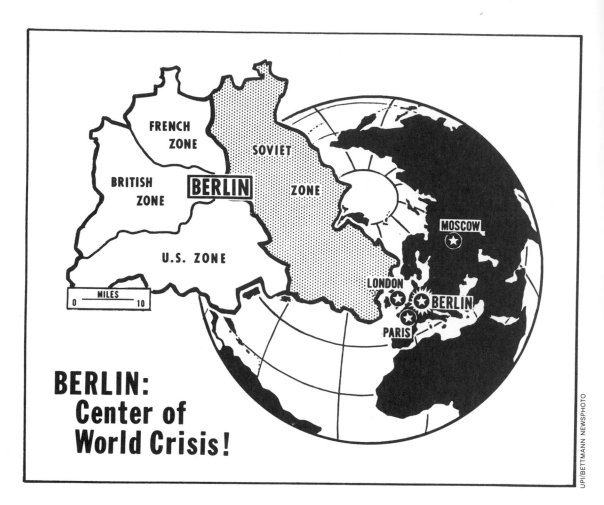

FRENCH ZONE

SOVIET

BRITISH ZONE

BERLIN

ZONE

U.S. ZONE

MILES
0   10

MOSCOW ✪

LONDON ★

BERLIN

PARIS ★

BERLIN: Center of World Crisis!

A map of Berlin, showing the divisions decided upon after World War II. Berlin was the focus of East-West tension after the East German authorities built the Berlin Wall to prevent citizens' leaving East Berlin. John XXIII's mediating words didn't resolve the crisis, but impressed Soviet leader Nikita Khrushchev.

In his very first radio address after his election as pope, he emphasized that his papacy would have two major themes — unity in the life of the Church and peace in the secular order. He was committed to bringing peace on earth to all men of good will. He knew that it was no small task — even for a pilgrim of peace.

During the early years of his papacy, John focused his energies on "Mater et Magistra," his encyclical on social order and government, and on planning the ecumenical council. Even though these activities were not direct overtures for world peace, they were contributions to improving relations among nations. By acknowledging the contributions of socialism to the life of mankind, Pope John reduced the tension that had existed up to that time between the Vatican and the communist nations of Eastern Europe. The ecumenical council, which brought together religious leaders from all over the world, improved ties between Eastern and Western nations.

But John's commitment to world peace went far beyond these two activities. As the pope during years of tense relations between the United States and the Soviet Union, John believed that it was crucial for him to take an active role in the peace process.

John had an important opportunity to get involved in the summer of 1961. The focal point of worldwide tension that summer was the city of Berlin, the former capital of Germany. Even though Berlin was a city in the heart of East Germany, a communist nation, the city had been jointly administered by American, British, French, and Soviet forces since World War II. The East Germans and their allies, the Soviets, wanted these other nations to leave Berlin, but they refused. The East German government was embarrassed by the large number of East German citizens who were leaving their country illegally through Berlin. Angry words were exchanged between President John F. Kennedy of the United States and Premier Nikita Khrushchev of the Soviet Union. Many people feared that there would be war over Berlin.

Pope John first spoke out on the Berlin crisis in a July address to "Pax Christi," a Catholic peace organization. His words captured the concerns of all the world. "The worries of fathers and mothers find an echo in our heart," he said. "And while we suffer from what is happening, we prefer to stress what unites and walk along the road with anyone as far as possible without compromising either justice or truth." It was an open invitation for the two sides to sit down with the pope to resolve their differences.

But the United States and the Soviet Union were not listening. When the Western nations refused to leave, the East Germans took action to stop the flow of refugees to the West. On the morning of August 13, East German construction crews began to build a wall that would permanently divide Berlin. From

Nikita Khrushchev at the Berlin Wall, erected suddenly on August 13, 1961. The normally suspicious Khrushchev trusted John XXIII because the pope's only motive was a sincere desire for peace, and he praised the pontiff in the Soviet newspapers.

that day on, no one could easily travel across the city. The world waited to see how the United States and its allies would respond.

Once again Pope John spoke out on the crisis. The world, he said, wanted peace and he appealed "to all our sons . . . to those who believe in God and His Christ, and also unbelievers, because all belong to God and His Christ, by virtue of their origins and redemption." This speech did not end the crisis, of course, but it did have an impact. Khrushchev was impressed by the pope's neutrality in the crisis. The Soviet premier told his associates that John was a man he could work with.

The United States took no action to tear down the wall or otherwise escalate the crisis. For its part, the East Germans and the Soviets dropped their demand that the Western nations leave Berlin. With a stalemate prevailing, the Berlin crisis faded from the pages of the press by December 1961. The wall remained, however, a symbol of the troubled relationship between East and West.

The crisis was also the beginning of a series of curious communications between the pope and the Soviet premier. On September 21, 1961, Khrushchev praised the pope and his efforts for peace in an interview published in *Pravda*, a major Soviet newspaper. "John XXIII pays tribute to reason," Khrushchev acknowledged. "From all parts of the world there rises up a desire for peace that we can only approve of. . . . It is not that we fear God's judgment, in which, as an atheist, I do not believe, but we welcome the appeal to negotiate no matter where it comes from." John responded by making discreet inquiries as to how relations between Moscow and the Vatican could be improved.

What was Khrushchev's motive for praising the pope? No doubt the premier wanted to divide the Western nations and depict the Soviet Union as the nation of peace. Some critics accused John of being naive for responding to this calculated flattery from Khrushchev. But John would not pass up any opportunity to work for world peace. He would willingly play the dupe if the end result was to ease world tension.

[The people] do not ask for those monstrous means of war discovered in our time, which cause fraternal and universal slaughter, but peace, that peace in virtue of which the human family may live freely, flourish and prosper.

—JOHN XXIII

Carlos Rafael Hablará en el 45 aniversario de la Revolución de Octubre
(Vea columna Ocho)

REVOLUCION

PRIMERA EDICION

(Acogido a la Franquicia Postal e Inscripto como Correspondencia de Segunda Clase.)

Año V   Nº 2103   La Habana, Lunes 5 de Noviembre de 1962   Director: Carlos Franqui ● 10 Centavos

¡PRIMERAS FOTOGRAFIAS DEL AVION YANQUI ABATIDO!

Restos del avión U-2, norteamericano, derribado sobre suelo cubano cuando espiaba. (Foto de la SECCION CINEMATOGRAFICA DEL MINFAR).

CONTINUAN HOY LAS CONVERSACIONES DE MIKOYAN

The first formal communication between the two men was an exchange of greetings on November 25, the pope's 80th birthday. Khrushchev telegrammed the birthday greetings of the Soviet people. John quietly responded with a telegram of good wishes to the premier, extending "to the whole Russian people cordial wishes for the strengthening of universal peace by means of understanding based on human brotherhood." A line of communication, however slender, now linked Rome and Moscow.

John had cause to use this line of communication a little less than a year later. On October 15, 1962, United States reconnaissance photographs proved beyond any doubt that the Soviets were building secret missile bases on Cuba, an island nation less than 100 miles south of the Florida coast.

For the previous three years the Soviets had been cultivating stronger economic and diplomatic ties with the communist government of Cuba and its leader Fidel Castro. Yet the world was shocked that

The wreckage of an American spy plane headlines a Cuban newspaper of November 5, 1961. One week earlier the Cuban Missile Crisis had ended when the Soviets agreed to remove their missiles from island. Khrushchev later called John XXIII's appeal to both sides "the only gleam of hope."

93

the Soviet Union would be so bold as to directly threaten the security of the United States. If completely operational, the missiles could destroy Miami, Atlanta, Washington, and other major American cities in a matter of minutes.

The presence of these missiles precipitated a second and far more serious crisis between the United States and the Soviet Union. President Kennedy was adamant that the missiles be removed, but Khrushchev refused to listen. On October 20 Kennedy ordered American war ships to blockade Cuba and turn back all Soviet ships attempting to enter Cuban territorial waters. As a convoy of Soviet cargo ships steamed toward Cuba, confrontation was only days away. Many feared that this conflict would lead to nuclear war and the end of the world.

Into the midst of this confrontation came the pilgrim of peace. On October 23 the pope received a request from President Kennedy to do what he could to lessen world tension. John's course of action was simple and direct. "I beg heads of state not to remain insensitive to the cry of humanity," he telegrammed

U.S. President John F. Kennedy informs the nation on television that the United States was blockading Cuba in response to the construction of Soviet missile bases. On October 23, 1961, John XXIII received a message from Kennedy asking the pope to do whatever possible to lessen world tension.

AP/WIDE WORLD

Fidel Castro, the communist leader of Cuba. He was insulted that the Soviet Union had not included him in strategy discussions before its decision to back down in the Cuban Missile Crisis.

to Khrushchev. "Let them do all that is in their power to save peace; in this way this they will avoid the horrors of war, the appalling consequences of which no one could predict. Let them continue to negotiate." John repeated these phrases in a radio broadcast to the world later that day.

There is no doubt that this message was heard in Moscow. The October 26 edition of *Pravda* carried a front page story on the speech under the headline, "We beg all rulers not to be deaf to the cry of humanity." Two days later Khrushchev took action to end the confrontation. The Soviet convoy would not attempt to break the blockade, work on the missile bases would be suspended, and the missiles would be removed. The world breathed a little easier.

How important was the pope's telegram to Moscow? "The pope's message," Khrushchev noted later to reporters, "was the only gleam of hope." It is likely that the telegram was the excuse that Khrushchev needed to back down from a confrontation that the Soviet Union did not want. By responding to the pope's message, Khrushchev could once again claim to be a man of peace.

The resolution of the Cuban Missile Crisis was not

> *Why should the resources of human genius and the riches of the peoples turn more often to preparing arms—pernicious instruments of death and destruction—than to increasing the welfare of all classes of citizens and particularly of the poorer classes?*
> —JOHN XXIII

95

the end of John's efforts to promote world peace. He continued to take every opportunity to stress the importance of peace in his communications with world leaders. Just as importantly, John continued his efforts to improve Vatican relations with the Soviet Union. He hoped that these efforts would eventually lead to a face-to-face meeting with Khrushchev himself.

John's efforts for world peace were recognized in March 1963 with the announcement that he had been awarded the Balzan Peace Prize. The prize had been established by a self-made industrialist named Eugenio Balzan and the selection of the winner was made by an international committee of diplomats and scholars. John was particularly pleased that his selection had been unanimous — even the Soviet representatives had voted for him.

Vatican officials had mixed feelings about the award. Many felt that the pope should not accept an award for what essentially was his job. But John saw the prize as another opportunity to speak out for peace. Even though he was very ill, he attended the award ceremony at the palace of the president of Italy. It was a historic occasion for more than one reason. The pope was being recognized for his work on behalf of world peace. It was the first visit of a pope to the home of the Italian president. And sadly, it was the pope's last appearance outside of the Vatican before his death.

John's most significant contribution to world peace was a pastoral message. On Easter Sunday 1963 he released to the world his great encyclical, "Pacem in Terris" (Peace on Earth). It was an extension of his philosophy as first expressed in "Mater et Magistra."

John began the encyclical by talking about the importance of order, which he defined as an extension of the will of God. Order among human beings meant that each individual had corresponding rights and responsibilities. Above all, each person had the right "to worship God in accordance with the right of his own conscience and to profess his religion in public." Human order also meant that developing countries had the right to determine

John XXIII receives the Balzan Peace Prize from Italian President Antonio Segni on May 10, 1963. John said at the time, "Peace is a house — a house for everyone." He donated the $160,000 prize to a war relief organization.

"Pacem in Terris" (Peace on Earth), John XXIII's great encyclical on peace in the nuclear age, was released on Easter Sunday 1963. The encyclical called for conciliation among all people, placing peace above political differences.

their own futures without interference.

"Pacem in Terris" also reflected the pope's optimism about the future. Unlike the previous popes, who had frequently condemned modern ideas, John saw in the 20th century a real growth in mankind's respect for human dignity. He noted a "progressive improvement in the economic and social condition of working men." He applauded the "part that women are playing in political life and that women are gaining an increasing awareness of their natural dignity." Finally he was most pleased to find that "imperialism is rapidly becoming an anachronism" since "all people have either attained political independence or are on the point of obtaining it." These were all aspects to him of an improving human order.

Yet the pope was also a realist. He had learned firsthand that men often drove each other to the brink of destruction. In "Pacem in Terris," John articulated the fears and concerns of the whole world. "In this age, which boasts of its atomic power, it no longer makes sense to maintain that war is a fit instrument with which to repair the violation of justice." But how could mankind insure that another confrontation like the Cuban Missile Crisis would not arise?

Crisis could be prevented if the major powers committed themselves to the principles of international organizations such as the United Nations and its affiliate agencies. Founded in the aftermath of World War II, the United Nations was a forum for the peaceful negotiation of conflicts between all the nations of the earth. John prayed that negotiations would lead to treaties, that treaties would ban nuclear testing, that an end to testing would lead to a ban on weapons themselves, and finally, that the world would systematically disarm itself. It was a long slow process, John knew. But without this orderly procedure, the future of the world would always be at risk.

"Pacem in Terris" did not offer anything new or unusual in the world of ideas. All of it had been said before by other advocates of world peace. What made "Pacem in Terris" unusual was that these ideas were

A priest and companion read a report of "Pacem in Terris" in *L'Osservatore Romano*. The encyclical caused controversy for its mild stance on communism. John XXIII realistically felt that communists too had a role in maintaining world peace.

Hiroshima after the first atom bomb destroyed the city in 1945. "Pacem in Terris" included a plea for disarmament, and the debate goes on in the Church over whether nuclear weapons are immoral.

coming from the pope. Previous popes had called for peace, but they always qualified their proposals with conditions. Pius XII, for example, had rejected the United Nations because it was too secular, but John praised the organization for the good work that it did.

"Pacem in Terris" was not a partisan Catholic document. It was a plea for conciliation between fellow Christians, between Christians and non-Christians, between East and West, and between rich nations and poor nations. No previous encyclical had ever addressed itself to such a diversity of problems faced by such a large audience. In this sense, "Pacem in Terris" was a unique and perhaps revolutionary document.

Not surprisingly, the encyclical caught the world's attention. Many world leaders supported the pope in his call for disarmament. But other leaders, particularly those in Western nations, rejected the encyclical as naive. Did the pope really think that the Soviet Union would disarm itself? John was fooling himself if he thought that Khrushchev could be trusted. This criticism hurt John deeply. His message had been misunderstood, he thought. With the resurgence of the peace movement in recent years, however, "Pacem in Terris" has become a key document in church history. John died without ever learning of the true impact of his work.

"Pacem in Terris" was the culmination of a lifelong commitment to world peace. As far back as 1906 John committed himself to find unity "in the cooperation of all men for the common good, and in the mutual trust between all men and social classes." For 57 years John had worked to fulfill that goal. Perhaps his most eloquent definition of peace came at the time he received the Balzan Peace Prize. Peace, he concluded "is the arc which unites earth and heaven, but to rise so high it has to stand on four solid pillars — truth, justice, charity, and freedom." Coming only a few months before his death, this definition, along with "Pacem in Terris" constituted the epitaph of a pilgrim of peace.

In fact, true peace will not be given to citizens, peoples, or nations, unless it is first granted to souls; for there can be no exterior peace if it is not the reflected image of interior peace.
—JOHN XXIII

AP/WIDE WORLD

The United Nations in New York City. The UN was founded after World War II as a global forum for peaceful negotiation. Although Pius XII had disapproved of the UN's secular nature, the Vatican maintains an observer there, and John XXIII praised the UN's achievements.

Last Will and Testament

> *He lived in the presence of God with the simplicity of one who strolls along the streets of his native city.*
> —CARDINAL SUENENS
> remembering John XXIII

Pope John had been praying for a swift and happy death for many years. John sincerely looked forward to an eternity with God in heaven. But death did not come soon for this son of Sotto il Monte. At his 80th birthday, in November 1961, John was robust and he showed no signs of slowing down the pace of his work. In fact, he believed that God would allow him the time to complete all of his papal projects. Most particularly he was concerned about the fate of the council that he had struggled so hard to establish.

All of this was wishful thinking on John's part. Late in the summer of 1962, John began to suffer from chronic stomach problems. He suspected it was gastritis, a common medical problem in the Roncalli family. But a battery of medical tests revealed something much worse — stomach cancer. In the elderly, stomach cancer is slow to develop and is very painful, and it was at that time inoperable. Pope John knew that he had received news of his death. He also knew that he had been granted a few more months, perhaps a year — time he could use to establish his council and to work for world peace.

John XXIII's coat of arms, the privilege of every newly elected pope. The shield is a symbol of the Church's power to lead nations, even in war, and the Latin motto below it expresses John's lifelong creed — "Obedience and Peace."

John XXIII celebrates mass on his favorite feast day — Pentecost — in 1962. He would give his last blessing to the people of the world on Pentecost Sunday one year later: *"Ut unum sint"* — "That they may be one."

Newspaper reports of John XXIII's battle with cancer were displayed all over Rome during his final days. As the world watched, the pope rallied several times before giving his final blessing. He died June 3, 1963.

The news of the pope's cancer was not made public, and John suffered stoically throughout the fall. At the opening of the council on October 8 he appeared healthy and in good cheer. But the cancer began to take its toll by late November, and the pain was so severe that John was forced to his bed. The Vatican press office revealed for the first time that the pope suffered from chronic stomach problems. Even though the word cancer was never used, an ominous pall came over the council. The pope was 81 years old. How much longer could he last?

But John seemed to draw strength from his pain. He was determined to continue his work. With the conclusion of the first session of the council, John turned his attention to the peace encyclical, "Pacem in Terris." He worked with urgency. He knew that he had less than a year to live and that all papal projects stopped at the death of a pope. John had to live at least until Easter when "Pacem in Terris" would be finished.

It took an extraordinary amount of strength and determination to finish the encyclical. The pain grew worse throughout the winter months, but John offered up his suffering as penance for his sins. After the publication of the encyclical on the Monday before Easter, 1963, John's health began to deteriorate rapidly. Still he would not take to his bed. Throughout April and May he continued to receive visitors and conduct papal affairs. On May 11 he even mustered the strength to travel to the Italian presidential palace for the Balzan Peace Prize ceremonies. "Every day is a good day to be born," he was fond of saying, "and every day is a good day to die."

By May 23 John knew that the day of his death was very near. He was too weak even to say Mass. By the end of the month the internal bleeding and pain were almost constant. "Help me to die as a bishop and a pope should," he said calmly to his secretary. The secretary fell to his knees and wept.

But John had not given up. He had not ended his ministry. On the last day of May he offered a few words of advice to those who stood at his deathbed. "The secret of my ministry is that crucifix you see opposite my bed," he said. "Look at it and see it as I see it. Those open arms have been the program of my pontificate. They say that Christ died for all. No one is excluded from his love, from his forgiveness." To his last full measure of strength, John counseled his Church to work for and with all men and women of good will.

Even though John could barely speak above a whisper, the world heard his voice. Hundreds of thousands of people showed up each day in St. Peter's Square to conduct a vigil and pray for the pope.

> *The pastor goes before all, opens the gate, guides his flock to fruitful pastures, wears his life out on behalf of his flock.*
> —JOHN XXIII

A large crowd was present on the evening of June 3 when the fateful news came from the Vatican palace. Good Pope John, pastor of the modern world, had died.

Since John's death more than 20 years ago, historians have explored why this pope was so influential. All of his predecessors had aspired to be the world leader that John was. Yet no pope in modern history has been as influential as John XXIII. What was the secret of his success?

To a large extent, John's influence was an extension of his personality. He saw himself as an international, interfaith pastor, an instrument of God's presence in the world. It was an extremely ambitious job description, even for a pope. "The remarkable achievement of his personality," notes historian Paul Johnson, "was that he was able to persuade multitudes of people, including many millions of non-Catholics, to accept this definition of his office — largely because they accepted his capacity to fill it." Everyone seemed to trust Pope John, even though they had never met him.

Yet John's influence was very personal. It did not carry over to the institution of the papacy or to his successors. The world embraced John as a leader and a peacemaker, but remained suspicious of the Vatican. The popes who succeeded John discovered that the world often would not listen to them as it had to John.

Even death has not diminished John's influence within the Church. The principles that John professed during his papacy — collegiality, reconciliation and ecumenism — continue to be fundamental to the work of the Church today.

Collegiality was John's method of sharing responsibility and power. The Church's policies and problems were to be addressed by bishops, clergy, nuns, and lay people working together. John diminished the papal tradition that centralized power in the Vatican. Today, the work of the Church is charted by parish councils of lay people, diocesan senates of parish pastors, and national conferences of bishops, as well as by the Vatican.

Reconciliation was John's way of opening the

[The council of cardinals who elected John XXIII] wanted a pope who would modernize the Church without destroying it, and who could neutralize the Church's enemies without denouncing them.
—FRANCIS X. MURPHY
Catholic priest
and biographer

Mahatma Gandhi, Indian leader and apostle of peace. His name means "great soul," and he was revered around the world. Like Gandhi, John XXIII was concerned for the poor and the outcasts of society.

doors of the Church to all those who wished to return. Through the modernization of the liturgy and doctrinal reform, John invited former Catholics to return to the religion of their birth. To a remarkable degree he was successful; tens of millions of people have once again become participating Catholics. This program of reconciliation continues to be a major element of parish programs.

Ecumenism was John's method of reaching out to other Christian denominations to find a common bond. Throughout his career, and particularly during his papacy, John focused on the points of agreement between Catholics and non-Catholics. As pope he had the opportunity to repair some of the damage done to Christianity during the hundreds of years of conflict between various denominations. He wanted Christianity in general, and the Church in particular, to become a moral force within an increasingly secular society. This could only be done if Christian denominations stopped fighting among each other and directed their energies toward a common goal. Today, Catholics regularly work on interfaith conferences and commissions established to address social and moral problems.

How are we to judge Pope John both as a man and as a world leader? Like other men, he had his limitations. His journal is full of self-doubt and occasional despair. At best he was a mediocre diplomat, a poor administrator, and a naive judge of human behavior.

But his sincere love for all mankind attracted millions of Catholics and non-Catholics to accept John as their spiritual father. Like Mahatma Gandhi and Martin Luther King, Jr., John was a world leader without much temporal power. His power was in his words of advice and encouragement. Love one another, he said, repeating the advice that Jesus Christ had given to his apostles.

By any measure John was a productive world leader. His time in that capacity was brief — little more than four and a half years. But in that short time, he utterly changed Catholicism, a denomination that had barely changed in the previous four centuries. "On a wider stage," concludes Paul John-

> *If one could reduce it all to a few words, I think one might say that John XXIII was a man singularly natural and supernatural at the same time.*
> —CARDINAL SUENENS

AP/WIDE WORLD

son, "John demonstrated that a spiritual leader whose sincerity was self-evident, can still make the world pause and think, at least for a time. What more can fairly be demanded of a single individual, brought to prominence in the twilight of life and equipped with little more than a pulpit?"

Above all else John was a pastor. He constantly challenged his Church to reinterpret the gospels in light of the present. He fought ceaselessly against

Dr. Martin Luther King, Jr., black American leader who preached love, and followed Gandhi's teachings of non-violent resistance. Winner of the Nobel Peace Prize in 1964, Dr. King's death was mourned worldwide when he was shot in 1968 during the civil rights struggle.

Wreaths encircle the tomb of John XXIII in Rome. Christians, non-Christians, and people of all nations were saddened by the death of the pope, who had carried a message of peace to all corners of the globe.

the barriers that divided men from one another. He knew that these barriers were a threat not only to world peace, but also to mankind's eternal salvation. "Today more than ever," John counseled from his death bed, "we are called on to defend above all and everywhere the rights of the human person, and not merely those of the Catholic church. . . . It is not that the gospel has changed; it is that we have begun to understand it better."

This was John's last challenge to both his Church and his world. Mankind has continued the long struggle with the issues of human rights and world peace just as it did in John's time. But in this struggle, Catholics and non-Catholics alike can draw strength from the life and work of the simple peasant from Sotto il Monte. Good Pope John continues in spirit to guide all people of good will in their quest for justice and world peace.

IOANNES P.P. XXIII

Mass is celebrated in memory of Pope John XXIII during the second session of Vatican II. At the council's end, Paul VI participated with other religious leaders in an unprecedented interfaith prayer, a testament to John's ecumenical vision.

Further Reading

Abbott, Walter J., ed. *The Documents of Vatican II.* New York: America Press, 1966.

Bonnot, Bernard R. *Pope John XXIII: An Astute Pastoral Leader.* New York: Alba House, 1979.

Hales, E. E. Y. *Pope John and his Revolution.* London: Eyre and Spottiswoode, 1965.

Hebblethwaite, Peter. *Pope John XXIII: Shepherd of the Modern World.* Garden City, N.Y.: Doubleday & Co., Inc., 1985.

Holmes, J. Derek. *The Papacy in the Modern World.* New York: Crossroads Publishing Company, 1981.

John XXIII. *Journal of a Soul.* Garden City, N.Y.: Doubleday & Co., Inc., 1966.

———. *Letters to His Family.* New York: Harcourt Brace, 1965.

Johnson, Paul. *Pope John XXIII.* Boston: Little, Brown and Co., Inc., 1975.

Kaiser, Robert B. *Pope, Council, and World: The Story of Vatican II.* New York: Macmillan Publishing Co., Inc., 1963.

Rynne, Xavier. *Letters from Vatican City.* New York: Farrar, Straus and Company, 1963.

Trevor, Meriol. *Pope John.* London: Macmillan, 1967.

Chronology

Nov. 25, 1881	Born Angelo Giuseppe Roncalli in the village of Sotto il Monte in northern Italy
Nov. 1893	Enters the Catholic seminary at Bergamo
Aug. 10, 1904	Ordained a priest and becomes secretary to the bishop of Bergamo
1915–18	Italy enters World War I; Roncalli is drafted and serves as an orderly in a Bergamo hospital, eventually rising to the rank of lieutenant
Jan. 1921	Roncalli is named Italian director for the Society for the Propagation of the Faith, a missionary aid organization
Feb. 17, 1925	Elevated to the rank of archbishop and designated "apostolic visitor" to Bulgaria by Pope Pius XI
Dec. 1934	Transferred to Istanbul to become the apostolic delegate to Turkey and Greece
1941–44	Works to aid civilians and refugees, especially Jews, during World War II
Dec. 1944	Appointed papal ambassador to France by Pope Pius XII
Jan. 12, 1953	Elevated to the rank of cardinal
March 1953	Installed as archbishop and patriarch of Venice, Italy
Oct. 9, 1958	Pope Pius XII dies
Oct. 28, 1958	Roncalli is elected pope of the Roman Catholic church, and chooses the name "John"
July 15, 1961	"Mater et Magistra," Pope John XXIII's statement on the role of government, published
Oct. 1962	Pope John opens the Second Council of the Vatican, now known as Vatican II, to discuss the status of the modern Catholic church
	At American President John F. Kennedy's request, Pope John sends a telegram to Soviet leader Nikita Khrushchev to lessen the tensions caused by the Cuban Missile Crisis
Dec. 1962	First session of Vatican II closes
March 1963	Pope John XXIII is awarded the Balzan Peace Prize
June 3, 1963	Dies in Rome after a nine-month battle with cancer

Index

Timothy Walch is editor of *Prologue: Journal of the National Archives* and associate editor of *U.S. Catholic Historian,* the quarterly journal of the U.S. Catholic Historical Society. He received his B.A. from the University of Notre Dame and his Ph.D. from Northwestern University. His essays on the history of Catholicism have appeared in many journals including *The Catholic Historical Review, Momentum, Notre Dame Magazine,* and *Religious Education.*

Arthur M. Schlesinger, jr., taught history at Harvard for many years and is currently Albert Schweitzer Professor of the Humanities at City University of New York. He is the author of numerous highly praised works in American history and has twice been awarded the Pulitzer Prize. He served in the White House as special assistant to Presidents Kennedy and Johnson.